D0849136

The Essence and Value
of Democracy

The Essence and Value of Democracy

Hans Kelsen

Edited by Nadia Urbinati
and Carlo Invernizzi Accetti

Translated by Brian Graf

ROWMAN & LITTLEFIELD PUBLISHERS, INC.
Lanham • Boulder • New York • Toronto • Plymouth, UK

Published by Rowman & Littlefield Publishers, Inc.
A wholly owned subsidiary of The Rowman & Littlefield Publishing Group, Inc.
4501 Forbes Boulevard, Suite 200, Lanham, Maryland 20706
www.rowman.com

10 Thornbury Road, Plymouth PL6 7PP, United Kingdom

British Library Cataloguing in Publication Information Available

Library of Congress Cataloging-in-Publication Data
Kelsen, Hans, 1881–1973.
[Vom Wesen und Wert der Demokratie. English]
The essence and value of democracy / by Hans Kelsen ; edited by Nadia Urbinati and Carlo Invernizzi Accetti ; translated by Brian Graf.
pages cm
Translated from German.
Includes bibliographical references and index.
ISBN 978-0-7425-3303-5 (cloth : alk. paper)—ISBN 978-1-4422-2212-0 (electronic)
1. Democracy--Philosophy. I. Urbinati, Nadia, 1955– II. Invernizzi Accetti, Carlo, 1983– III. Title.
JC423.K37813 2013
321.8—dc23
2013024913

♾™ The paper used in this publication meets the minimum requirements of American National Standard for Information Sciences Permanence of Paper for Printed Library Materials, ANSI/NISO Z39.48-1992.

Printed in the United States of America

Contents

Editors' Introduction

Hans Kelsen is widely recognized as one of the most important legal theorists of the twentieth century.[1] His "pure" theory of law remains one of the essential points of reference for all contemporary debates on the nature of legal norms, constitutionalism, and international law.[2] Surprisingly, however, his political writings are not nearly as widely known as his legal theory, especially in the English-speaking world (as evidenced by the fact that this is the first published English translation of Kelsen's most important treatise on democracy, and also by the fact that many more of his seminal works on this topic remain to be translated). This is surprising for at least two reasons. First of all, Kelsen's writings on democracy constitute an important complement to his juridical work, and are therefore essential to understand both the content and the evolution of his thought as a whole. Secondly, the treatise here presented constitutes a major contribution to democratic theory in its own right, which is still worth studying today for the arguments and insights it develops concerning issues that remain central for contemporary politics. The principal purpose of this introduction is, accordingly, to substantiate these two claims.

The centrality of Kelsen's theory of democracy both for the evolution of his thought as a whole and for a proper understanding of his legal writings in particular can be brought out by situating it within the context of Kelsen's overall intellectual trajectory and its relation to the broader historical and political concerns of the time. *The Essence and Value of Democracy* was first published in 1920, and then again in a much revised and expanded edition (the basis for the present translation) in 1929. At the time, Kelsen's reputation as a prominent legal scholar had already been largely established, following the publication of his *Hauptprobleme der Staatsrechtslehre* in 1911. Moreover, in the aftermath of World War I, Kelsen had been directly involved in the drafting of Austria's first "democratic" constitution, under which he served as permanent judge in the newly established constitutional court throughout the 1920s.

1

In this context, it was immediately clear to constitutional and political theorists of his time that Kelsen's treatise on democracy constituted an attempt to spell out and defend the normative principles underscoring his conception of the constitutional order. Indeed, Kelsen's identification as a "left-leaning liberal"[3] theorist of law was so uncontroversial at the time that he could afford to recognize it explicitly. In a later redacted passage from the preface to the first edition of his *Hauptprobleme der Staatsrechtslehre* he had, for example, written that: "because in this my results coincide with much of the classical tradition of the liberal conception of the state, I could not object if anyone wanted to see in my work a symptom of that new form of liberalism that nowadays appears to be spreading everywhere."[4]

The political content of Kelsen's legal theory only really began to appear problematic toward the end of the 1920s and the beginning of the 1930s, when the ideal of parliamentary democracy began to be called into question in Europe. The intensification of the so-called crisis of parliamentary democracy was a consequence of the radicalization of the conflict between the parties of the revolutionary proletariat and the reactionary bourgeoisie on one hand, and the power of civil law and of social and ideological loyalties on the other hand. It prompted Kelsen to insist more and more on the "purity" of his conception of the legal order: a movement which culminated with the first publication of his *Pure Theory of Law* in 1934, in which the link with any substantive set of political values is explicitly disavowed.[5]

In this sense, far from corresponding to a retreat from the domain of the political, Kelsen's insistence on the "purity" of his theory of law may be interpreted as a political strategy in itself. For, to assert the political independence of the constitutional conception of the legal order in the face of the multiple challenges that were raised against it by revolutionary bolshevism, the Catholic movement, and the incipient fascist movements, constituted a way of reasserting its capacity to deal with the mounting crisis in a peaceful and democratic way, since its implication was that it would not be necessary to overthrow the existing constitutional structure for the contending parties to achieve their goals. From this perspective, the insistence on the "purity" of the legal order therefore constituted a political defense of the democratic system, inasmuch as ideological neutrality with respect to the political projects that take shape within its framework is one of the distinctive features of liberal democracy itself.

As Matthias Jestaedt aptly wrote, Kelsen's theory of "purity" was able to break two taboos at once: on the one hand, it took away from the judicial practice the veil that concealed the undisturbed action of politics; and on the other, it overcame the traditional fetters that prevented the judicial organs of the state from making or justifying political decisions. The "purity" of the legal order was a way to make this order at once politically active and responsible. For this reason, in Kelsen's doctrine, the purity of the law and democracy go hand in hand as two "complementary" autonomies.[6]

This link was perfectly evident to all the most important participants in the public debate at the time, and in particular to Kelsen's critics and antagonists, such as, most notably, Carl Schmitt, perhaps the most radical anti-Kelsenian thinker of his time. In his *Constitutional Theory* (first published in 1928) Schmitt interchangeably treats Kelsen both as a "liberal theorist of the *Rechtstaat*" and as a defender of "constitutional democracy."[7] In addition, as many subsequent commentators have pointed out, the famous exchange between Kelsen and Schmitt on the seemingly purely "juridical" topic of Article 48 of the Weimar constitution was at core a debate about the political form of democracy, since it culminated in a disagreement over the respective roles of the presidency and the constitutional court in relation to the parliamentary system.[8] Indeed, it was a general feature of the German-language debate on the so-called crisis of parliamentary democracy in the 1920s and 1930s to treat issues of public law and political form as reciprocal extensions of each other.

It was therefore only after Kelsen's emigration to the United States in 1940 that the intimate connection between his legal theory and his political philosophy started to be obscured. In part, this was certainly due to Kelsen's own increasing focalization on the juridical aspect of his work, and in particular on the attempt to formulate a consistent theory of international law in the aftermath of World War II. In addition, however, it should also be pointed out that the intellectual climate in the United States was particularly unfavorable to an adequate reception of Kelsen's political theory as an inseparable complement to his theory of law.

Since the Cold War was dominated by the ideological confrontation between a form of liberalism conceptually grounded on the notion of "natural law," and the Marxist critique of constitutional democracy as merely "formal," there was not much conceptual space left for a theory of democracy resolutely challenging the premises of *both*. Moreover, throughout the 1950s and early 1960s, American political science departments were dominated by a form of methodological behaviorism which severely restricted the scope for normative political theory itself, due to its insistence on the purely "scientific" and "non-evaluative" dimensions of the discipline. As a consequence, the article Kelsen published in 1955 in the journal *Ethics*, in which he explicitly reformulated and further expanded his theory of democracy for an English-speaking audience,[9] failed to generate much interest and debate, and has been largely ignored both by the secondary literature on Kelsen's work and by Anglo-American theorists of democracy in general.

Paradoxically, it has been this selective reading of Kelsen's work—disproportionately focused on his "juridical" writings, and taking the idea of axiological "purity" out of its historical context—that has generated many of the most tenacious misconceptions about it, such as the idea that Kelsen's thought is "abstract," "formalistic," and "severed from reality."[10] Quite to the contrary, what emerges from an analysis of his intellectual trajectory is that all of Kelsen's works were developed in response to concrete political problems of the time; and, more specifically, that his legal and political writings were never meant to be kept separate, but rather emerged in conjunction with each other, for the purpose of consistently advancing a distinctive set of political values.

These last remarks bring us to the second reason why it may appear surprising that Kelsen's writings on democracy are not nearly as well-known as his juridical ones in the English-speaking world: that they are not only essential for understanding Kelsen's thought, but also constitute an important contribution to the history of democratic theory in their own right, and still retain many important lessons and insights for political theory today. From this point of view, *The Essence and Value of Democracy* can be read as one of the most rigorous and compelling attempts available to apply the founding values of the great "democratic" revolutions of the eighteenth and the nineteenth centuries—which Kelsen refers to from the first lines of the text[11] —to the specific historical context of modern industrial societies.

As such, this text constitutes a systematic reconstruction of the self-understanding of most existing democratic regimes, first and foremost in continental Europe, but also, in a more indirect way, in the Anglo-Saxon world. For this reason, its interest from the point of view of contemporary political theory is neither merely descriptive nor antiquarian: it also implicitly offers a standard against which existing regimes can be evaluated; or, to put it differently, a sort of "mirror" in which contemporary societies can see themselves reflected in a way that opens up the possibility of assessing the state and quality of their own democratic institutions.

Such a work of self-reflection appears particularly necessary today, and Kelsen's text particularly well-suited for serving as its basis, because (despite the obvious differences in both nature and intensity) a number of significant parallels can be drawn between the situation in which Kelsen first began to develop his theory of democracy and the one we are experiencing today. As was the case then, in fact, the ideal of parliamentary democracy appears to have become today the object of much dissatisfaction and even radical critiques. On one hand, the left of the political spectrum laments its "formality' and incapacity to achieve meaningful social reform (witness the calls for more "direct" forms of political representation and so-called substantive democracy). On the other hand, the political right increasingly challenges parliamentarism in the name of a stronger and freer "executive power" (as testified by the widespread longing for forms of presidentialism), "social unity" (i.e., the need to control social conflict, especially in relation to the economic crisis), and the "epistemic" quality of its political decisions (i.e., the role of "independent authorities" such as judges and experts in the political process).[12]

Since Kelsen's text was originally written as a response to a similar set of multiple and interlocking challenges, as well as a "mirror" for contemporary societies, it can also serve as an "arsenal" of arguments for the political and intellectual project of *defending* parliamentary democracy against its contemporary critics. In the remaining part of this introduction, we shall therefore spell out some of these arguments, as a way of underscoring the contemporary relevance of Kelsen's text for the ongoing debate on the nature and value of the democratic form of politics and government.

The first point that appears worth noting is that Kelsen provides a defense of parliamentary democracy based primarily, if not exclusively, on the principle of *freedom*, which Kelsen understands in terms of the concept of "autonomy." Indeed, as he would later make much clearer in his *General Theory of Law and State*, Kelsen's theory of democracy is inscribed within an overall typology of political regimes that makes the concept of "autonomy" into the defining criterion of the most basic political distinction. For him, democracies are predicated on the idea that coercive legal norms are only legitimate to the extent that those who are subjected to them have contributed to making them, while all other political regimes are predicated on a principle of "authority," which ultimately involves a measure of heteronomy.[13] Kelsen thereby situates his theory of democracy within a typological dualism that reminds us of Immanuel Kant's distinction between regimes that are legitimate (i.e., republican, constitutional, and representative) and regimes that are autocratic: in both cases, freedom constitutes the essential criterion in relation to which regimes are evaluated.[14]

This point is extremely important because it sets itself in stark contrast with two other grounds from which the legitimacy of democracy is sometimes deduced: on one hand, the idea of "equality"; and on the other hand, the "epistemic" quality of political decisions. To be sure, the first of these points is not meant to suggest that Kelsen's theory of democracy is opposed to, or even incompatible with, the recognition of the value of political equality. On the contrary, Kelsen's deduction of the constitutive features of parliamentary democracy from the principle of collective autonomy supposes the recognition of the legal and political equality of individual citizens.

However, the reason why it is important to distinguish his theory from those that attempt to ground the legitimacy of democracy on equality alone is that this usually serves the purpose of contrasting the merely "formal" conception of equality implicit in the idea that everyone should have an equal right of participating in the process of collective self-government, to a more "substantive" conception of equality supposedly taking into account the extent to which the objective interests of all those concerned are actually reflected in the actual political outcomes. This dualism can also be interpreted in two opposite but parallel ways. Liberals would use it to claim, critically, that democracy has primarily to do with equality and may thus be unfriendly to liberty. Socialists would use it to claim that true democracy requires more than legal and political equality not to be merely procedural. Kelsen tried to rebut both distorted views by pointing to the fact that a substantive conception of equality leads to a conceptual separation between the idea of government "for" the people and "by" the people, which ultimately has the effect of *opposing* the concept of equality to that of freedom.

It was for example a common line of argument amongst Marxists in Kelsen's time (which also persists, in different forms, amongst contemporary theorists seeking to ground political legitimacy on the notion of "justice"[15]) to claim that "real" democracy does not depend as much on the process through which collective decisions are made, but rather on the extent to which the outcome fulfills certain basic interests of human beings. In this respect, Kelsen points out that all really existing forms of government claim to be exercised "for" the people. However, since there is no objective standard against which this interest can be measured, the only thing that can distinguish democratic government from all others is that it is also government "by" the people. In other words: that the people are the only ultimate judge as to what constitutes "justice" in the first place.

From this point of view, arguments contrasting "formal" and "real" democracy are revealed to be covert critiques of democracy itself, inasmuch as they betray mistrust in the people's capacity to do what is best for them, if given the opportunity to govern themselves. For Kelsen, on the other hand, "formal" and "substantive" democracy are "inseparable from one another," inasmuch as the former constitutes the only available means for realizing the latter:

> The demand for preferably universal, and therefore equal, free-dom requires universal, and therefore equal, participation in government. . . . Insofar as the idea of equality is meant to con-note anything other than formal equality with regard to freedom (i.e., political participation), that idea has nothing to do with de-mocracy. This can be seen most clearly in the fact that not the political and formal, but the material and economic equality of all can be realized just as well—if not better—in an autocratic-dicta-torial form of state as it can in a democratic form of state.[16]

A parallel argument is also advanced by Kelsen with respect to the idea, already common in his time, which has been recently taken up and greatly expanded by so-called epistemic theories of democracy, according to which the legitimacy of democratic regimes can be derived from the fact that they are supposedly capable of producing the "best" kinds of political decisions. [17] This view is different from the old Platonist kind of "epistocracy" or technocracy inasmuch as it seeks to sever the link between the idea that there exists an objec-tive political "truth" and the claim that political decisions should therefore be entrusted to the individuals who are reputed most "competent" in discovering it, by suggesting that expanding the pool of decision-makers is more likely to generate outcomes that approximate the presupposed objective standard of normative "truth."

What Kelsen's insistence on the constitutive link between free-dom and democracy reveals, however, is that this line of argument ultimately ends up perverting the normative grounds for the legitimacy of democracy by introducing a form of technocratic logic at its very core. For, the assumption that there exists an objective standard of political "truth" implies that the ultimate *ends* of political action are not up for being defined or renegotiated by the people themselves. Thus, the reference to a normative criterion of "truth" ultimately displaces the significance of the notion of "autonomy" as the grounds for political legitimacy, which is what Kelsen seems to be suggesting when he writes that attempts to justify democracy on the basis of the "epistemic" quality of its political decisions ultimately make it appear as a "donkey in a lion's skin."[18]

On this basis, Kelsen further claims that grounding political legitimacy on the principle of autonomy only really makes sense if we suppose that an objective standard of political "truth" is not available. That is, in other words, that the legitimacy of democratic autonomy is inextricably tied with the presupposition of a form of philosophical "relativism" as a background epistemic standpoint.[19] From a historical point of view, this claim can be interpreted as a way of asserting that democracy is the specific kind of political regime that best suits the fact that, at least within the context of modernity, all the previous "epistemic" grounds for justifying political authority have been called into question. As Kelsen himself puts it: "He who in his political desires and actions is able to lay claim to divine inspiration or otherworldly enlightenment may well be right to be deaf to the voices of his fellows." However, "he who views absolute truth and absolute values as inaccessible to human cognition must deem not only his own but also the opinion of others as at least feasible . . . The idea of democracy thus presupposes relativism as its world-view."[20]

Another way of stating the same point is that for Kelsen, democracy is the most appropriate kind of political regime for dealing with a historical situation in which an irreducible form of *pluralism* (or what Weber called "polytheism of values"[21]) has replaced the previous philosophical and metaphysical consensus on the grounds for political authority. Given these background philosophical and sociological premises, Kelsen claims that freedom—that is, the idea of collective self-government on the basis of mutual equality—is the only legitimate grounds on which coercive laws can be justified. A systematic separation and even opposition is therefore set up between "freedom" and "truth" as the respective philosophical grounds for political legitimacy within modernity, and assumed to correspond to the basic political distinction between "democracy" and "autocracy."

Together with his reassertion of the value of "freedom" as the principal foundation for democracy, the second set of distinctive features of Kelsen's theory springs from his defense of "parliamentarism" as the most appropriate means to realize the ideal of autonomy in contemporary societies. This notion is defined in Kelsen's work as the conjunction between two distinct political techniques: on one hand, political representation, which implies that collective decisions are to be taken by a specialized body of government whose members are chosen through election by those to whom the decisions are supposed to apply; and, on the other hand, the majority principle as a decision-making rule to be employed within this elected body.

The argument Kelsen provides to justify these two political techniques is essentially the same: that even though each represents a "compromise" with respect to the abstract ideal of popular sovereignty, they are both necessary for constructing a form of government that approximates the abstract ideal of autonomy in the conditions of modern industrial society. Since, however, each version of the argument touches upon a specific set of issues that are central to the contemporary debate on parliamentarism, we shall briefly comment on them in turn.

With respect to the principle of political representation, Kelsen claims that the attempt to institutionalize a form of "direct" democracy at the level of contemporary political units would actually result in a system that is *less* democratic than parliamentarism. This is because modern industrial societies are based on the principle of the division of labor, which implies that not all citizens could meaningfully participate in a universal deliberative assembly. As a consequence, Kelsen suggests that large scale plans for "direct" democracy have the more immediate effect of masking rather than abolishing concrete relationships of power, and actually promote rather than prevent the formation of ruling elites.[22]

Conversely, the specific advantage of political representation, for him, is that it makes the relationships of power that inevitably develop within large and complex political communities into a specific object of political deliberation, and therefore opens them to the possibility of being peacefully renegotiated by the citizens themselves. This shows that Kelsen's defense of the principle of political representation is not based on what he calls the "fiction" that political representatives somehow "reflect" or "embody" the views and interests of the political collectivity as a whole. Kelsen is fully aware that the relationship of representation is a relationship of power; however, the claim he makes for it is that it provides means for those upon whom power is exercised to select—and change—those who exercise it.

In this respect, it is interesting to point out that Kelsen even goes as far as to suggest that the idea according to which political representatives can somehow "reflect" or "embody" the views and interests of those they are supposed to represent may actually play into the hands of the *critics* of parliamentary democracy, inasmuch as it furnishes them with the argument, common since the times of Joseph de Maistre, that "democracy is based on a palpable lie."[23] This can be interpreted as a strategy of "deflation," intended to defend parliamentary democracy against these potential critics by situating the link with freedom at a more "indirect" level, in the measure of "control" exercised by citizens over their representatives through the mechanism of elections, rather than in the overblown idea of a "direct" exercise of political power by the people over themselves.

In this sense, Kelsen's theory may appear to have something in common with the early versions of "procedural" or "realist" theories of democracy that had already begun to be articulated in Kelsen's time by authors such as Gaetano Mosca and Joseph A. Schumpeter, and have recently been taken up and further expanded by "minimalist" theorists such as Adam Przeworski, William H. Ricker, and Richard Posner.[24] It is important to point out, however, that there are relevant differences between Kelsen's political thought and this strand of democratic theory. As a matter of fact, Kelsen is not willing to sever the link between democracy and freedom and to concede to the idea that democratic elections are simply a method for changing the elite without jeopardizing peace. On the contrary, Kelsen insists all the mechanisms through which elections enable citizens to have an "indirect" influence on political decisions, besides allowing for a peaceful substitution of leaders. This shows that Kelsen's goal is not peace alone, in the tradition of Thomas Hobbes, but peace along with freedom, in the tradition of Immanuel Kant. The reconciliation of the requirements of "peace" with those of collective "freedom," through the establishment of a practical link between them, can therefore be understood as one of the distinctive features of Kelsen's theory of democracy.[25]

This is reflected also in the argument Kelsen advances in defense of the majority principle, which is pitted against the idea that "unanimity" or "consensus" are required to ensure that the decision reflects the wills of those who are supposed to be represented in it. In this respect, Kelsen points out that a requirement of unanimity would actually deprive collective decisions of their coercive character, and therefore rid them of all political significance, whereas majority rule is said to "maximize" the number of individuals who can be considered free within the framework of a coercive social order, while assuming that everybody is of equal moral value.[26]

To understand the logic of this argument, it is essential to take into account that Kelsen inscribes his defense of the majority principle within an overall temporal framework of continuity, involving the possibility of *revising* previously approved decisions, as well as formulating new ones. For, once this possibility is introduced, it ceases to be the case that unanimity implies that all individuals must necessarily agree with the collective decisions in effect. On the contrary, what unanimity means is that, in principle, even a single individual could prevent the existing set of decisions from being altered. Thus, according to this method, the minority (and potentially even the single individual) has the last word, not the majority. For this reason, democracy cannot be grounded on unanimity.

The majority principle, on the other hand, ensures that more individuals are in favor of the existing social order than opposed to it at any given time. It is in this sense that Kelsen claims that majority-rule "maximizes" the number of individuals who can be considered free within it: "Anything less would mean that the will of the state could from its very inception conflict with more wills than it agrees with. Anything more would make it possible for a minority, rather than the majority, to determine the will of the state by preventing an alteration of that will."[27]

From the point of view of the ongoing debate on the merits of parliamentarism, this argument can be interpreted as a way of converting what has traditionally been identified as one of the greatest "weaknesses" of this political form into one of its "strengths." For, an objection that has often been raised against parliamentary procedures, both in Kelsen's time and ours, is that they are *indecisive* and time consuming, and therefore incapable of making the hard choices that may be required, especially during times of political crisis.[28] Against this objection, Kelsen's response is to point out that, precisely because it does not claim to "embody" the people as a whole, or approximate some context-transcending idea of "truth," but only to produce a series of "compromises" that reflect the underlying views and interests of the people represented in it, the great advantage of parliamentarism is that it can always revise previous decisions, as soon as these underlying views and interests change.

Although this does not mean that parliamentarism will always produce the "best" political decisions, it does mean that it has the merit of being able to correct its decisions, since the recognition of its own fallibility is inscribed within the defense of the majority principle itself. Political instability within a regulated framework is therefore rescued from the prevailing assumption that it is necessarily something "bad." On the contrary, Kelsen's argument reveals that it can reflect the greater capacity of a political system to adapt to shifting political circumstances, compared for example to a system in which the leaders claim to embody a higher authority, derived from a principle of absolute political "truth."

What we have in front of us are therefore two interpretations of what a democratic society is and should look like. One is based on an open process making and remaking decisions in a climate of freedom and contestation. The other aims instead to overcome the fatal partiality of decisions that are achieved by many conflicting minds into a unified ideal (the truth) or one person (the popular leader). In Kelsen's times as in ours, this antithesis seems to pertain to the way of interpreting democracy as either a process or as an achieved fact. Kelsen teaches us that interpreting democracy as a process is a more faithful approach to the democratic promise since its inception in ancient Athens: the promise of allowing individuals who are different in social conditions and value orientations to give themselves laws that treat them as equal in legal and moral dignity. This, for him, is the real mission of democracy, not the achievement of some good or correct outcome, and not even the unification of the masses in the image of a single "body" that one leader or one vision pretends to embody.

The third aspect of Kelsen's theory of democracy that is worth highlighting from the point of view of contemporary debates within the field of political theory is its defense of the role played by political parties and proportional representation within the parliamentary framework. This stems directly from Kelsen's rejection of the idea of representation as an "embodiment" of the political unity of the people. Kelsen asserts that the idea of a unified and homogenous "people" as the sociological substrate of democracy is a metaphysical abstraction. Instead, he takes modern societies to be characterized by irreducible conflicts both at the level of material interests and individual worldviews, and for this reason posits parliamentarism as the means for enabling these conflicts to be played out peacefully, in search of collective decisions that satisfy at least the majority, while giving the minority the hope of being able to become a majority.

Within this framework, political parties are assumed to exercise an essential function as mediating organs between individual views and interests and the policies that can be put into effect at the level of the state, inasmuch as they serve to aggregate individual preferences and give them the possibility of concretely affecting the political decisions that are made in parliament. Kelsen writes:

> It is a well-known fact that, because he is unable to achieve any appreciable influence on government, the isolated individual lacks any real political existence. Democracy is only feasible if, in order to influence the will of society, individuals integrate themselves into associations based on their various political goals. Collective bodies, which unite the common interests of their individual members as political parties,8 must come to mediate between the individual and the state.[29]

On this basis, Kelsen further asserts that criticisms of the political party as an organizational form (which were as common in Kelsen's time as they are in our own[30]) constitute "an ideologically veiled resistance to the realization of democracy itself,"[31] inasmuch as they challenge the practical means through which citizens can exercise a direct influence on political decisions, but also, more fundamentally, because they represent an attack on the legitimacy of political conflict and, therefore social division, itself. This is very clear, for example, in the context of Kelsen's exchange with Carl Schmitt on the concept of "the guardian of the constitution," during which the latter defended the political role of the presidency as an instance of government that could "stand above" partisanships expressed in the parliament. For Kelsen, on the other hand, politics *is* partisanship, and the political party is the only organizational instance that can reflect this at the level of government.[32] In this sense, the ultimate "guardian of the constitution" is the very open process of partisanship that characterizes the political life of free and equal citizens, inside and outside the parliament. Thus democracy preserves itself by manifesting its conflictual character and allowing the actors to achieve temporary compromises and decisions according to rules and procedures all citizens accept and comply with.

For this reason, in *The Essence and Value of Democracy*, Kelsen also makes a number of interesting proposals for strengthening the role of political parties within the framework of existing parliamentary regimes, many of which retain much of their innovative value today. First of all, he suggests that the party form should be given a legal basis within the constitution itself (something that was later put into effect in Germany by the Basic Law of 1948, but which remains an exception with respect to most other democratic constitutions). Secondly, he suggests that political representation within parliament could cease to be tied to specific individuals, by granting parties the possibility of revoking the mandate of representatives, so as to give them a more direct control over the way political decisions are actually taken.[33]

The party thereby becomes an intermediary body that plays two crucial roles. As in the liberal tradition, it protects the collective decision-making system from its own majoritarian power by injecting pluralism within it; and, as in the democratic tradition, it protects the citizens from the power that representative institutions exercise over them by providing them with the means to control it. The party can impose a kind of political mandate on its representatives that, without having any legal validity, contributes in making the electors more than a merely appointing authority. By itself a controlling and checking authority, it allows citizens to exercise their influencing power over time. In this sense, the party makes the representative system possible, insofar as it actualizes the normative conditions through which the representatives do *not* replace the citizens in the work of decision making, but share with them in the complex process of making collectively binding decisions.[34]

From this point of view, it is also interesting to consider the defense Kelsen provides of the system of "proportional" representation of political parties within the parliament. This is pitted against two competing alternatives that were already being discussed in Kelsen's time, but remain highly pertinent, albeit in different forms, today: on one hand, systems of "corporatist" representation, which aim to give expression to specific professional and economic interest groups in the decision-making body; on the other hand, "majoritarian" or "first-past-the-post" systems of electoral representation, based on territorial districts. Although the issues at stake in the two cases are slightly different, the argument Kelsen advances in defense of proportionality against both these alternatives is based on the same principles, so it is worth considering them in conjunction.

With respect to "corporatist" representation, Kelsen points out that it relies on the presupposition that all individual interests and worldviews correspond to those of one's profession or economic class. While this may have been a tolerably accurate assumption in the case of pre-modern or *ancien régime* societies—which were still based on "organic" estates that pre-assigned a specific place and function to their members within the social whole—it has become totally inappropriate in the context of modern societies, which are based on individual rights and social differentiation of functions, both of which are in turn predicated on the principle of individual free choice. The reason is that this specifically modern form of individualism opens up the possibility of overlapping cleavages and conflicts of interest within existing economic and professional classes. [35]

As a consequence, Kelsen claims that the only way to give an adequate expression to the multiplicity of conflicting views and interests that develop in modern societies is to allow individuals themselves to determine their own political affiliations through the mechanism of voluntary association—which is the basis of the modern political party. This translates into a conception of the party system as a system of political alliances that is constructed from the "bottom-up"; that is, within society as it understands itself and for the purpose of influencing the state, rather than ascriptively or on the basis of a set of professional categories that are determined in advance.

For Kelsen, this "bottom-up" logic virtually implies a system of "proportional" representation, because this is the system that allows for the greatest variety of competing interests and worldviews to be represented in parliament, as well as the greatest flexibility in the creation of new party organizations. The same principle therefore also underscores his critique of "majoritarian" or "first-past-the-post" systems. First of all, Kelsen points out that these systems still implicitly rely on an "arbitrary" criterion for the aggregation of individual preferences, since the territorial districts within which votes are counted cannot be determined by the electoral process itself and must therefore be defined ascriptively in advance. [36] In addition, Kelsen notes that "majoritarian" systems also imply that a very large proportion of the votes that are actually cast (indeed, potentially even the majority, depending on how districts are apportioned) do not obtain any representation at all within parliament.

On the contrary, the great advantage of proportional representation, for Kelsen, is that it implies that *all* the different constellations of interests and worldviews that obtain a sufficient number of votes can be represented in parliament:

> In the ideal case there are no losers in a proportional vote, because no majorities are formed. . . . [Accordingly] one could say that this representation has come about with the votes of all and against the votes of none. Of course, this only applies to the ideal case. As a general rule, there will in fact be minorities who fail to obtain the minimum number of votes necessary to win a seat and, thus, go unrepresented. However, the higher the number of open seats in relation to the number of votes cast . . . [constitutes a greater approximation to] the aforementioned fundamental principle . . . of freedom, i.e., of radical democracy. Just as I only want to obey a law, which I have helped create, so I only want to recognize someone—if anyone at all—as my representative in government, if he was chosen for this position by, and not against, my will.[37]

This last passage clearly shows that Kelsen's defense of proportional representation is based on the same underlying argument as his defense of parliamentarism in general: that it constitutes the most appropriate means for constructing a form of government that approximates the abstract ideal of popular sovereignty in the conditions of modern industrial society. From this point of view, parliamentarism and a multi-party system based on proportional representation therefore prove to be inseparable from each other as the concrete manifestation of democratic self-government in modern society.

Finally, the last distinctive element of Kelsen's overall theory of democracy that appears worth pointing out in the present context is its inextricable interconnection with the principle of constitutionalism, which Kelsen notoriously understands as a criterion of legal validity positing that legal norms can be considered valid only if they have been created in conformity with the procedures stipulated by "higher" norms.[38] This point rejoins and complements the one we already sought to establish in the first part of this introduction; for, just as there it was a matter of showing that the implicit political content of Kelsen's theory of law is spelled out in his writings on democracy, what we will attempt to bring out now is that, for Kelsen, democratic self-government is possible only within the framework of a constitutional order displaying the distinctive features of the system outlined in his juridical writings.

At core, this connection stems from Kelsen's rejection of what he calls the "metaphysical" conception of the "people" as a reified sociological entity existing independently of the legal order. For him, the "people" can only really be understood as a purely artificial entity, defined by the legal norms as the set of individuals to whom it is supposed to apply. From this it follows that democratic self-government cannot take place within a hypothetical "state of nature": since the "people" is an inherently juridical entity, it requires a set of legal procedures to determine how it can express itself and, therefore, govern. Accordingly, the legal order does not need to be understood as an independent set of constraints, imposed "externally" on the exercise of popular sovereignty, but emerges instead as its background condition of possibility. In other words: Kelsen's point is that democratic self-government is possible only within the framework of a constitutional order, because this is what defines the procedures that enable the people to govern themselves in the first place. In this sense, one might say that the democratic process itself is a form of constitutionalized politics, inasmuch as rules and procedures are essential for making it work.

This point appears significant from the point of view of the contemporary debate on the relation between democracy and constitutionalism because it implies that Kelsen's theory of democracy is not vulnerable to the standard "liberal" (and "conservative") objection according to which popular sovereignty is a dangerous principle because it contains no inherent "limits" to the power that may be legitimately exercised by the "people" over themselves (and may therefore run the risk of converting into a form of "tyranny"[39]). Inasmuch as it is assumed to be possible only through a set of juridical procedures, Kelsen's theory of democracy proves to contain the resources for limiting the exercise of political power within itself, because the very same procedures that make the expression of the popular will possible in the first place also function as limits on what it can legitimately be. Thus, in a sense, Kelsen's conception of popular sovereignty can be said to be limited *by the logic of its own exercise*.

This shows that, as well as being inherently "constitutional," Kelsen's theory of democracy is also inherently "liberal," in the sense that it does not need to import the grounds for limiting its own exercise of political power from outside, but contains them already inscribed within its own institutional framework.[40] That this must necessarily take the form of a "hierarchical" system of norms whereby the production of ordinary legislation is constrained by a requirement of consistency with a "higher" set of principles inscribed in the constitution is then further demonstrated by Kelsen through an argument advanced specifically in response to the objection that the adoption of the majority principle as a decision-making rule could result in an abuse of power over the minority.

The starting point is the claim that a democratic majority cannot afford to annihilate the minority, or even alienate it to such a point that it ceases to participate in government, because "that would deprive it of its own character as a majority" and therefore of its democratic legitimacy.[41] From this, Kelsen deduces that a proper institutionalization of the majority principle itself supposes the recognition of certain "fundamental rights" guaranteeing not only the continued existence but also the active participation of the majority in the political process.

In turn, from this the only way of making these rights juridically effective is to inscribe them within a constitutional order that is not itself immediately accessible to the possibility of being changed or nullified by the elected majority. Thus, the conclusion reached is that the proper institutionalization of the majority principle requires the introduction of certain "super-majoritarian" constraints, which constitute the basis for a distinction between different "levels" of legislation, according to the kelsenian conception of the legal order as a "hierarchical" system of norms that "regulates the mechanism for its own production."

This is recognized explicitly by Kelsen in *The Essence and Value of Democracy* when he writes that: "The protection of the minority is the essential function of so-called freedoms and fundamental rights or human and civil rights, which are guaranteed by all modern parliamentary-democratic constitutions. . . . The typical way of qualifying constitutional laws vis-à-vis conventional laws is the requirement of a higher quorum and of a special—possibly two-thirds or three-quarters—majority."[42] Thus, far from being incompatible with the value accorded to the majority principle, Kelsen's defense of the principle of constitutionalism ultimately turns out to be a necessary condition for its realization in the first place.

From this perspective the limits imposed on simple majorities in parliament are to be interpreted as limits that the democratic constitution poses on the elected. Accordingly, they are not meant to protect only the elected minority in parliament but all the citizens at large, by imposing limits on what representatives in parliament can do. As a complement to majority rule, super-majoritarian constraints make sense because democracy is actualized in indirect or representative form. This has the effect of tying Kelsen's theory of democracy to the notion of constitutionalism by a double knot: not only as its implicit political content, but also in the sense that the latter constitutes the necessary institutional framework of the former.

To conclude, Kelsen's treatise can therefore be said to provide a complex and articulate defense of constitutional democracy as a multifaceted political ideal, which involves a number of interrelated features: individual political rights, parliamentarism, majority-rule, proportional representation, and an essential role for political parties, as well as an overall constitutional structure imposing specific limits on the democratic exercise of state power. All these distinctive features are "deduced," in one way or another, from the practical conditions required to realize the abstract ideal of popular sovereignty in the conditions of modern industrial society, but they also prove to be reciprocally sustaining, and in some cases even practically necessary for each other. The overall system that emerges from this analysis is therefore that of an integrated "system" that Kelsen proposes as a sort of *practical ideal* for the concrete realization of democracy in contemporary societies, which as we said can serve both as a "mirror" for contemporary democracies to see their state and condition and as an "arsenal" of arguments for defending themselves from their critics.

BIOGRAPHIC NOTE

Hans Kelsen was born in Prague on October 11, 1881. When he was three years old, his mother, Auguste Löwy (from Bohemia) and his father, Adolf Kelsen (from Galicia), moved to Vienna, then the capital of the Austro-Hungarian Empire, where the family started a small business in the production of chandeliers (which would not survive the economic crisis that followed World War I). In his autobiography, Kelsen spoke of his youth as absorbed in writing poems (some of which were published in a popular magazine) and reading literature. When the time for choosing his career came, he decided to study jurisprudence because, he confessed, he didn't want to end up teaching in a high school. He graduated from law school in 1906, having already published his first book on Dante Alighieri's doctrine of the state the year before.

Unlike his professional vocation, which was steady and fixed, his religious and political loyalties changed several times, by either choice or necessity. Kelsen was born a Jew, but converted to Catholicism in 1905 and to Protestantism in 1912 (the year he married Margarete Bondi, who also converted). He was an Austrian citizen, but also acquired Prussian citizenship in 1930. Six years later, he was deprived of all of them for racial reasons and thus acquired Czech citizenship. Finally, he became an American citizen in 1945 and remained so until his death in Berkeley in 1973.

After his doctoral studies in Vienna, Kelsen was a visiting student in Heidelberg and Berlin. In 1911, he obtained the qualification to teach public law and philosophy in Vienna, where in 1917 he became an associate professor and in 1919 a full professor. After his work on Dante, he concentrated on the study of the theory of law and in 1911 published his first major work, *Hauptprobleme der Staatsrechtslehre entwickelt aus der Lehre vom Rechtssatze*. This work made the important claim that law is constituted by a system of norms, and that any theory of right must accordingly be a theory of norms, from which it followed that even the so-called will of the state is in fact a fiction covering up something more difficult to understand: that the norm is by itself devoid of any voluntaristic element.

Kelsen's theoretical frame was characterized by a dualistic scheme, like subjective law and objective law (on the basis of which he would develop his criticism of *ius naturale* doctrine) and private law and public law. His life task was devoted to criticizing the mixing of legal philosophy with sociology and psychology or with the normative political postulates concerning the doctrine of the state and sovereignty. The methodological opposition between *Sein* (is) and *Sollen* (ought), inspired by Immanuel Kant's philosophy and the renaissance of neo-Kantianism under the leading role of Wilhelm Windelband and then of Hermann Cohen, the founder of the Marburg neo-Kantian school, was therefore at the source of Kelsen's idea of "purity," without which juridical science (and justice) could not be autonomous.

Alongside his academic career, Kelsen also played a seminal political role in Austria as the inspirer of constitutional parliamentary democracy. Facing the decline of the Imperial structure of the state, as a researcher and advisor in the Ministry of War, he first had the opportunity to draft a plan for the transformation of the Imperial monarchy into a federation of nationalities in 1914. In it, he proposed replacing the Emperor with a collegial council of representatives appointed by each nationality. The Emperor, Kelsen recalls, was too late in evaluating this plan and when he decided to endorse it; his role was already too compromised on the international scene, forcing him to resign.

After the war, in the fall of 1918, Kelsen was directly involved in drafting the new constitution of the Austrian state, which in his mind should have been a federation in the form of representative democracy. He tried to follow the model offered by the Weimar constitutional order then under discussion, but made some radical changes that reflected his democratic orientations: the president of the Austrian federation was to be elected by the Federal Assembly (the parliament) not by the people directly, he was not the leader of Army (a task of the National Council), and moreover did not have the power of proclaiming a state of emergency. Most importantly, the juridical kernel of Kelsen's proposal lay in the constitutional oversight of the political and administrative systems by a Constitutional Court, of which he was to be nominated first as a member in 1919 and then as a member for life in 1920.

During his term of service as a constitutional judge, Kelsen directly experienced the detrimental effects of a politicization of the constitution. In connection with a case concerning the issue of divorce, over which the Catholic Church mobilized strongly, Kelsen became the object of a public smear campaign intended to undermine his credibility as a judge and force him to resign. This fed into rising demands for a reform of the Constitutional Court intended to limit its independence by making it more directly accountable to the elected majorities in parliament. Kelsen denounced the proposal as a threat to the stability of the democratic regime and when it was finally passed through a constitutional amendment supported by the fascist and the Christian Social parties in 1929, he resigned from his position.

Soon after, Kelsen left Vienna for Cologne, where he taught from 1929 to 1933. Yet his position both in the academy and the country became difficult and dangerous. He then accepted a teaching appointment in Geneva and Prague (the latter did not last more than a few semesters because of the violent attacks of the Nazi youth movement against Jewish professors). Kelsen increasingly felt that his life and that of his family (he had two daughters) were at risk, and therefore decided to leave Europe.

While teaching in Prague, he had received a *laurea ad homorem* from Harvard University. Soon after, the president of the New School for Social Research, Alvin Johnson, offered him a teaching position, which helped him obtain a visa to enter the country. However, Kelsen did not accept the New School's offer and instead took up an Oliver Wendell Holmes Lectureship at the Harvard Law School. With his family, he left Geneva in June 1940; they reached Lisbon, passing through Zurich, Locarno, and Barcelona, and embarked on June 1st on the ship S.S. Washington, which arrived in New York eleven days later.

Once in America, Kelsen soon moved to Berkeley, although he could not teach in the University's Law School as he would have preferred. Instead, he was hired by the Department of Political Science. He became a full professor of international laws and jurisprudence in 1945, the very same year his *General Theory of Law and State* was published. After the war, in 1947, the University of Vienna awarded him a further *laurea honoris causa*. The autobiography he wrote in 1947 ends with Heine's words on his grave in Montmartre: "While I am writing these memoires I became sixty-six. From the wide window close to my desk I can see, beyond the garden, the Bay of San Francisco and the Golden Gate, beyond which the Pacific Ocean shines. Here I will have 'the last rest of the tired traveler.'"

NOTES

1. The curator of his autobiographical writings observed that if there had been a Nobel Prize for jurists, Kelsen would have deserved one. Cf. Matthias Jestaedt, *Einleitung*, to the out-of-print edition of *Hans Kelsen in Selbstzeugnis* (2006), quoted from the Italian translation in Hans Kelsen, *Scritti autobiografici*, ed. Mario G. Losano (Reggio Emilia: Diabasis, 2008), p. 36.

2. For a comprehensive overview of the debate surrounding Kelsen's legal philosophy, see Stanley Paulson, "Hans Kelsen and Normative Legal Positivism," in *The Cambridge History of Philosophy 1870 – 1945*, ed. Thomas Baldwin (Cambridge: Cambridge University Press, 2003). See also *Law, State and the International Legal Order : Essays in Honor of Hans Kelsen*, ed. Engel Salo (Knoxville: University of Tennessee Press, 1964), and the special section entitled "The Pure Theory of Law: A Tribute to Hans Kelsen," published by the *California Law Review* 59, no. 3 (1971).

3. Cf. Paolo Petta, "Presentazione" in Hans Kelsen, *Il Primato del Parlamento* (Milano: Giuffré, 1982). On this point see also Maurizio Barberis, "Introduzione" in Hans Kelsen, *La Democrazia* (Bologna: il Mulino, 1995).

4. Hans Kelsen, *Hauptprobleme der Staatsrechtslehre* (Tubingen: JCB Mohr, 1911), p. 8 (as quoted by Barberis, "Introduzione," p. 13; our translation).

5. Cf. Hans Kelsen, *Pure Theory of Law*, Berkeley: University of California Press, 1967, pp. 1–4.

6. Cf. Jestaedt, *Einleitung*, in Kelsen, *Scritti autobiografici*, p. 37.

7. Cf. Carl Schmitt, *Constitutional Theory*, trans. Jeffrey Seitzer, foreword by Ellen Kennedy (Durham, NC: Duke University Press, 2008), pp. 63–64 and 280.

8. On this point, see for example Peter Caldwell, *Popular Sovereignty and the Crisis of German Constitutional Law: The Theory and Practice of Weimar Constitutionalism* (Durham, NC: Duke University Press, 1997); and David Dyzenhaus, *Legality and Legitimacy: Carl Schmitt, Hans Kelsen, and Hermann Heller in Weimar* (Oxford: Oxford University Press, 1999).

9. Hans Kelsen, "Foundations of Democracy," *Ethics*, vol. 66 (1955), pp. 1–101.

10. In 1964, for example, Judith Shklar identified Kelsen as one of the main exemplars of a specific kind of "legalistic" ideology, which in her opinion was guilty of obscuring the political content implicit in the very idea of a "neutral" constitutional order; Judith Shklar, *Legalism: Law, Morals and Political Trials* (Cambridge, MA: Harvard University Press, 1964), pp. 29–39.

11. Cf. *Infra.*, p. 25.

12. For a comprehensive summary systematizing these several lines of critique see Robert Dahl, *Democracy and Its Critics* (New Haven, CT: Yale University Press, 1991).

13. Cf. Hans Kelsen, *General Theory of Law and State*, trans. Anders Wedberg (London: Transaction, 2008) (originally published by Harvard University Press, 1945), pp. 284–303.

14. Cf. Immanuel Kant, *The Metaphysics of Morals* (Cambridge: Cambridge University Press, 1996).

15. On this point, see for example Philippe Van Parijs, *Real Freedom for All* (Oxford: Clarendon Press, 1995) and Thomas Pogge, *Freedom from Poverty as a Human Right* (Oxford: Oxford University Press, 2007).

16. Cf. *Infra.*, p. 97.

17. See for instance David Estlund, *Democratic Authority: A Philosophical Framework* (Princeton, NJ: Princeton University Press, 2008); Susan Stokes, "A Rational Theory of Epistemic Democracy," paper presented at the Yale-Oslo conference *Epistemic Democracy in Practice*, October 20–22, 2011; and Hélène Landemore, "Democratic Reason: The Mechanism of Collective Intelligence in Politics. Collective Wisdom. Old and New," in *Collective Wisdom. Principles and Mechanisms,* Hélène Landemore and Jon Elster eds. (Cambridge: Cambridge University Press, 2012).

18. Cf. *Infra.*, p. 102. On this point, see also Kasper Lippert-Rasmussen, "Estlund on Epistocracy: A Critique," *Res Publica* 18, no. 3 (2012).

19. Cf. *Infra.*, p. 103.

20. Cf. *Infra.*, pp. 103–104.

21. For a systematic discussion of the conceptual links between Max Weber and Hans Kelsen, see Carlos-Miguel Herrera, *Le Droit, le Politique. Autour de Max Weber, Hans Kelsen et Carl Schmitt* (Paris: l'Harmattan, 1995).

22. Cf. *Infra.*, p. 41.

23. Cf. *Infra.*, p. 50.

24. For a comprehensive review of this literature, see Adam Przeworski, *Democracy and the Limits of Self-Government* (New York: Cambridge University Press, 2010).

25. On this point, see Philippe Raynaud, "Introduction" in Hans Kelsen, *La Democratie: Sa Nature et sa Valeur* (Paris: Dalloz, 2004).

26. Cf. *Infra.*, p. 1. See also Infra., pp. 67–76.

27. Cf. *Infra.*, p. 31.

28. Perhaps the most famous version of this objection is the one provided by Carl Schmitt in his book on *Political Theology*, where he suggested that a liberal-democrat is one who would answer the question "Christ or Barabbas?" with "a proposal to adjourn or appoint a commission of investigation"; Carl Schmitt, *Political Theology* (Chicago: University of Chicago Press, 1985), p. 62. For a more contemporary version of an analogous argument, see also Harvey Mansfield, *Taming the Prince: The Ambivalence of Modern Executive Power* (New York: Free Press, 1989).

29. Cf. *Infra.*, p. 39.

30. On this point, the classic text is of course Robert Michels, *Political Parties: A Sociological Study of the Oligarchical Tendencies of Modern Democracies* (New Brunswick, NJ: Transaction, 1962); for a more recent discussion, see also Giovanni Sartori, *Parties and Party Systems* (Cambridge: Cambridge University Press, 1976).

31. Cf. *Infra.*, p. 39.

32. Cf. Kelsen's review of Schmitt's book on *The Guardian of the Constitution*, which is still not translated in English, but is available in German in Hans Kelsen, *Wer soll der Hüter der Verfassung sein?* (Tubingen: Mohr Siebeck, 2008).

33. Cf. *Infra.*, pp. 60–61.

34. Cf. Nadia Urbinati, *Representative Democracy: Principles and Genealogy* (Chicago and London: University of Chicago Press, 2006), pp. 35–39, 130–35.

35. Cf. *Infra.*, p. 64–65.

36. Cf. *Infra.*, pp. 70–71.

37. Cf. *Infra.*, pp. 71–72.

38. Kelsen, *General Theory of Law and State*, p. 122.

39. The most famous formulation of this argument is of course contained in Alexis de Tocqueville's *Democracy in America*. However, for more recent formulations of the same basic concern, see Frank Cunningham, *Theories of Democracy: A Critical Introduction* (New York: Routledge, 2002). For a similar argument based on different conceptual premises, see also Josef Ratzinger, *Values in a Time of Upheaval* (San Francisco: Ignatius Press, 1996).

40. Although this is not stated explicitly in *The Essence and Value of Democracy*, it was later formally recognized by Kelsen in his article on the "Foundations of Democracy," where he writes that: "Modern democracy cannot be separated from political liberalism. Its principle is that the government must not interfere with certain spheres of interests of the individual, which are to be protected by law as fundamental human rights or freedoms. It is by the respect of these rights that minorities are safeguarded against arbitrary rule by majorities." Hans Kelsen, "Foundations of Democracy," *Ethics*, vol. 66 (1955), pp. 27–28.

41. Cf. *Intra.*, p. 69.

42. Cf. *Infra.*, pp. 67–68.

Preface

The bourgeois revolutions of 1789 and 1848 made the democratic ideal an almost self-evident fact of political discourse. Even those who wanted to prevent its realization to some degree still paid deference to it in principle or carefully masked their endeavors with democratic terminology. In the decades before the Great War, no important statesman or noteworthy literary figure could be said to show an open and candid commitment to autocracy. Indeed, despite that period's growing class tensions, there exists no disagreement between the bourgeoisie and the proletariat with regard to the democratic form of state; on this point, liberalism and socialism do not differ ideologically. Democracy is the catchword that has almost universally dominated the minds of the nineteenth and twentieth centuries.

Precisely for this reason, however, democracy—like every catchword—has begun to lose its precise meaning. Since it has become politically fashionable to utilize this catchword for all purposes and occasions, this most abused of all political concepts has taken on diverse, and often contradictory, meanings—that is, if brainless, vulgar political rhetoric has not already degraded it to a meaningless, conventional phrase.

Now, the social revolutions triggered by the [First] World War compel a revision of even this political value. Before, the [resulting] powerful movement of the masses had aimed with the greatest energy for democracy, which next to socialism—as the name of the leading party attests—constitutes half of that movement's theoretic foundation. Now, however, at precisely the moment when it should be realizing not only its socialist, but also its democratic tenets, that movement has splintered. One of the resulting two parts has continued—first hesitatingly and then again with renewed decisiveness—in the old direction. The other, meanwhile, is pushing resolutely and turbulently towards a new goal, which unabashedly reveals itself as a form of autocracy.

But it is not only the dictatorship of the proletariat—theoretically justified by a neo-communist doctrine and practically realized by the Bolshevik Party in Russia—that threatens democracy. The tremendous pressure exerted by this proletarian movement on the thinking and politics of Europe has also resulted in an anti-democratic response on the part of the bourgeoisie. This response finds its theoretic as well as practical expression in Italian Fascism. Hence, just as it was previously confronted with monarchic autocracy, democracy today is faced with challenges from party dictatorships on both the Left and the Right.

ONE

Freedom

In the idea of democracy—and for the moment this, not its relative approximation in political reality, shall be our topic of discussion—two postulates of our practical reason are united and two primitive instincts of man as a social being strive for satisfaction. First and foremost, there is the reaction against the coercive nature of the social condition: the protest against the subjection of one's own will to the will of another and the resistance to the agony of heteronomy.

Nature itself demands freedom and, thus, rebels against society. The more one man's primary feeling of self-worth depends on the rejection of any other man's higher worth, the more he perceives the foreign will, which the social order imposes upon him, as a burden. The more elementary the relationship between the subject and the master, the more likely the former is to ask: "He is a man like me; we are equal! What gives him the right to rule over me?" Thus, the thoroughly negative and deeply antiheroic[1] idea of equality comes to justify the similarly negative demand for freedom.

The assumption that we are equal in principle may seem to imply that no man has a right to rule over another. Yet experience teaches us that if we want to remain equal in reality, we must allow ourselves to be ruled. Nonetheless, political ideology insists upon combining freedom and equality, and precisely the synthesis of both principles is characteristic of democracy. Cicero, a master of political ideology, expressed this in the famous statement: "*Itaque nulla alia in civitate, nisi in qua populi potestas summa est, ullum domicilium libertas habet: qua quidem certe nihil potest esse ducius et quae, si aequa non est, ne libertas quidem est*" (Freedom has its seat only in a state where supreme power is with the people and there can be nothing more pleasant than that freedom, which is no freedom at all if it is not equal).[2]

The only way for freedom to enter into the calculus of social and even political organization—which it, after all, rejects—is by undergoing a change in meaning. Instead of negating social order in general and the state in particular, freedom must come to embody a particular form of these. And this form, democracy, together with its dialectical opposite, autocracy, then represents all possible forms of state and, indeed, of society in general.

For society and the state to be possible, there must be a valid normative order regulating the mutual behavior of men, i.e., there must be rule. But if we must be ruled, then we only want to be ruled by ourselves. Natural freedom is transformed into social or political freedom. To be politically free means to be subject to a will, which is not, however, a foreign, but rather one's own will. The fundamental conflict underlying forms of state and of society is therefore established.

From an epistemological standpoint, if one wishes to differentiate society as a coherent system from nature, one has to be able to provide the former with an ordering principle similar to that of the latter.[3] The norm emerges as a counterpart to the law of causality. Natural freedom originally negates the social order, while social freedom, as the idea of free will, negates the causal order. The slogan "back to nature (or natural freedom)" expresses the desire to be free from social constraints. Conversely, "toward society (or social freedom)" expresses the demand to be free from causal necessity. This contradiction is only resolved, once the idea of "freedom" comes to embody a particular, namely social (i.e., ethical-political and legal), ordering principle, once the conflict between society and nature comes to be viewed as a conflict between two different ordering principles and so two different [epistemological] schemes of interpretation [*Betrachtugsrichtungen*].

Freedom in the sense of the political self-determination of the citizen, of participation in government,[4] is usually identified as a classical idea. As such, it is contrasted with the Germanic idea of freedom, which connotes freedom from domination and from the state as a whole. In fact, this difference is not historically or ethnographically accurate. Rather, the move from the Germanic to the so-called classical conception of freedom is only the first step in an inevitable process of transformation ("denaturing"), which the original instinct to be free undergoes as human consciousness moves out of the state of nature and into the coercive social order.

This change in the meaning of the idea of freedom is extremely characteristic of the mechanics of our social thinking. The extraordinary importance, which this idea has in political ideology, is only explicable if the idea is seen as originating from deep within the human soul and from a primitive instinct, which is antagonistic toward the state and places the individual in conflict with society. Yet, through an almost puzzling act of self-deception, the idea of freedom is transformed into nothing more than the expression for the specific social position of the individual. Anarchical freedom becomes democratic freedom.

The change is more profound than it might appear at first sight. Rousseau, possibly the most important theorist of democracy, formulates the problem regarding the best constitution, which, from his point of view, is the problem of democracy,[5] in the following way: "To find a form of association which may defend and protect with the whole force of the community the person and the property of every associate, and by means of which each, coalescing with all, may nevertheless obey only himself, and remain free as before."[6] Rousseau demonstrates just how important freedom is to his political system when he decries the parliamentary principle in England: "The People of England regards itself as free; but it is grossly mistaken, it is free only during the election of members of parliament. As soon as they are elected, slavery overtakes it, and it is nothing."[7]

Consequently, Rousseau advocates the principle of direct democracy. Even if the ruling will of the state is formulated by direct popular vote, however, the individual is free only at the moment he casts his vote, and even then only if he votes with the majority, not if he belongs to the overruled minority. Thus, the democratic principle of freedom appears to demand that the possibility of being overruled be minimized: a qualified majority and possibly even unanimity are required as guarantees for individual freedom. Given that practical politics are defined by conflicts of interest, however, such guarantees are so implausible that even a radical apostle of freedom like Rousseau requires unanimity only for the original contract that initially creates the state.

Nor is the restriction of the unanimity principle to the hypothetical founding of the state merely, as is so often assumed, a matter of expediency. For if the principle of freedom requires unanimity for the conclusion of the original contract, then, strictly speaking, it follows that one should also require the unanimous consent of the

subjects as a condition for the continuous validity of the order created by that contract. This would mean that everyone would be free
to leave society and withdraw from the binding force of the social
order at any moment by simply refusing to recognize the legitimacy
of that order. This consequence clearly reveals the incompatibility
that exists between the idea of individual freedom and the idea of
social order. Such an order, by its very nature, is possible only if its
validity is objective, i.e., ultimately independent of the will of those
subject to that order.

Even if the content of the social order is in some way determined
by the wills of the subjects, the objective validity of that order remains intact from a specifically social standpoint. Still, formal objec-
tivity requires a substantive equivalent. In the extreme case, where
the "you ought" of the social imperative depends on the "when and
whatever you will" of the individual it is addressed to, the order no
longer has any social meaning. If society and the state are to be
possible, then one must be able to differentiate between the content
of the order and the will of the individuals subject to it. If the tension between the two poles of *ought* and *is* is zero and the value of
freedom infinitely great, then subjection becomes impossible. Since
a democratic social order, which was hypothetically founded upon
a unanimous contract, can be further developed via majority decisions, it contents itself with a mere approximation of the original
idea of freedom. The fact that one still speaks of self-determination
and of everyone only being subject to his own will, even when the
will of the majority is binding, represents another step in the metamorphosis of the concept of freedom. [8]

Yet, not even the individual who votes with the majority is subject only to his own will. He becomes immediately aware of this fact
when he changes the will expressed in his vote. The fact that a
change in his individual will is legally irrelevant shows clearly that
he is subject to a foreign will or, formulated without the use of a
metaphor, to the objective validity of the social order. He is free
again only if the change in will is confirmed by a majority. The more
qualified the majority required to bring about a change in the ruling
will of the state, the more difficult is the achievement of a concordance between that will and the will of the individual and the less
effective is the guarantee for individual freedom. If unanimity were
required, this concordance would be practically impossible.

Here, a strange ambiguity in the political mechanism is revealed.
The same principle, which first protected the freedom of the individual during the establishment of the social order, now enchains

him when he is no longer able to withdraw from that order. The original creation of the social order or of the government is not, after all, part of our social experience. The individual is usually born into an already established social order, in the creation of which he did not participate. Thus, he is confronted with a foreign will from the very beginning. Only the alteration, the development, of the social order is practically in question. And from this perspective, the principle of an absolute, not a qualified, majority represents the relatively greatest approximation to the idea of freedom.

It is from this idea, and not—as is often thought—from the idea of equality, that the principle of the majority is derived. The majority principle certainly presupposes the equality of human wills. But this equality is only a metaphor. It cannot connote the ability to effectively measure and add those human wills. It would be impossible to justify the majority principle by saying that more votes carry a greater total weight than fewer votes. The purely negative assumption that the will of one person should not count more than the will of another does not entail the positive claim that the will of the majority should rule. A majority principle derived from the idea of equality would actually have the mechanical, even senseless, character attributed to it by the autocratic critique of democracy. It would simply be the poorly formalized expression of the experiential fact that the many are stronger than the few. The proposition that "might goes before right" would only be overcome insofar as this idea were elevated to the level of a legal norm.

Instead, the only sensible premise for the principle of the majority is the idea that, if not all, then at least as many individuals as possible should be free. This means that the number of individual wills that are in conflict with the general will of the social order should be minimized. The fact that not just this or that individual— since one is not worth more than another—but rather that the greatest possible number of individuals should be free shows that equality constitutes an essential postulate of democracy. Under these circumstances, the fewer wills one's own has to agree with in order to effect a change in the will of the state, the easier it is to achieve a concordance between the individual will and the will of the state. Here, then, an absolute majority does in fact constitute the upper limit. Anything less would mean that the will of the state could from its very inception conflict with more wills than it agrees with. Anything more would make it possible for a minority, rather than the majority, to determine the will of the state by preventing an alteration of that will.

The meaning of freedom has changed from the idea that the individual should be free from state rule to the idea that he should be able to participate in that rule. This transformation simultaneously requires that we detach democracy from liberalism. Since the demand for democracy is satisfied insofar as those subject to the order participate in its creation, the democratic ideal becomes independent of the extent to which that order seizes upon them and interferes with their "freedom." Even with the limitless expansion of state power and, consequently, the complete loss of individual "freedom" and the negation of the liberal ideal, democracy is still possible as long as this state power is constituted by its subjects. Indeed, history demonstrates that democratic state power tends toward expansion no less than its autocratic counterpart.[9]

A discrepancy between the will of the individual, with whom the demand for freedom originates, and the political order, which confronts the individual as a foreign will, is unavoidable. This is even true of democracy, where this difference is only approximately minimized. Hence, the notion of political freedom is transformed still further. Individual freedom, which is basically impossible to achieve, fades into the background and the freedom of the social collective comes to the fore. The resistance against being ruled by one's peers leads to an unavoidable shift in what political consciousness perceives as the ruling Subject: [it leads] to the anonymous personification of the state. It, rather than actual human beings, is seen as exercising dominion. A mysterious collective will and an almost mystical "collective person" are differentiated from the wills and personalities of individuals.

This fictitious insulation occurs not so much with respect to the wills of those subject to the order, but rather the wills of the individuals who in fact exercise power, yet now appear as nothing more than organs of a hypostatized ruling Subject. In an autocracy, the ruler may be deified, but he is nonetheless a man of flesh and blood. In a democracy, the state as such appears as the ruling Subject. Here, the veil of state personification conceals the factual rule of man over man, which is so intolerable to democratic sensibilities. Without a doubt, the personification of the state as a basic idea of constitutional legal theory has its roots in this democratic ideology as well.

Once the idea of being ruled by one's peers is abolished, however, one is no longer shielded from the realization that the individual, insofar as he must obey the state order, is not free. With a shift in [the identity of] the ruling Subject comes a shift in [the identity of] the Subject of freedom. Even greater emphasis comes to be placed on the idea that the individual, insofar he creates the state order in organic relation with other individuals, is "free" in this and only this relation. The Rousseauean notion that the subject surrenders his freedom entirely in order to regain it again as a citizen is so telling, because this differentiation between subject and citizen reflects the total change of social perspective—the complete shift in the formulation of the problem—involved here. The subject is the isolated individual of an individualist social theory, while the citizen is the dependent member of a collective, only a part of a larger organic whole, within a universalistic social theory. From the valuative standpoint of freedom, which is necessarily individualistic, [however,] the idea of a collective has a metaphysical and transcendent character.[10]

The perceptual shift is so entirely complete that it is basically no longer correct, or at least no longer important, to claim that the individual citizen is free. Some authors have correctly concluded that, since citizens are only free through the state that embodies them, it is not the individual citizen, but the personified state that is free. The same thing is expressed by the proposition that only citizens of a free state enjoy freedom. Individual freedom is replaced by popular sovereignty, and a free state, or republic [*Freistaat*], becomes the fundamental demand.

This, then, is the last step in the transformation of the idea of freedom. Those who are either unwilling or unable to trace this movement, which the concept—driven by its own immanent logic—undergoes, may well get caught up in the apparent contradiction between the original and final meanings. They also forgo the ability to comprehend the conclusions drawn by democracy's most ingenious theorist. Rousseau was not afraid to conclude that a citizen is only free through the general will, and that, as a result, anyone who refuses to obey this will can, by forcing him to obey, be forced to be free. It is more than paradoxical—it is symbolic of democracy—that in the Genovese republic the word "liberty" could be read over prison doors and on the chains of galley slaves.[11]

NOTES

Notes from the translator for all chapters are indicated in brackets.

1. Koigen, *Die Kultur der Demokratie* (1912), p. 4.
2. [Translation is Kelsen's own from Kelsen, "Foundations of Democracy," in *Ethics* 66, no. 1, part 2, p. 18.]

3. [I have used both "ordering principle" and "order" to translate the German *Gesetzlichkeit*.]

4. [German: *Mitwirkung an der Bildung des herrschenden Willens im Staate.* Literally, this means "participation in the creation of the ruling will of the state." Here and throughout most of the book, I translate this, as well as other similar phrases or words connoting the same idea (e.g., *Gemeinschaftswillensbildung* and *Staatswillensbildung*), as "government," because it provides a much simpler and succinct translation, while retaining essentially the same meaning Kelsen intends. In some instances, where accuracy or context demand it, I have used the literal translation instead. However, *Gemeinschaftswillen* and *Staatswillen* by themselves have always been translated literally as "will of society" and "will of the state," respectively.]

5. Of course, this is not an impartial way of formulating the problem. When inquiring into the nature of democracy, one cannot begin by presupposing that it constitutes the best form of state. This appears to be the problem with Steffen's otherwise excellent exposition on the matter (*Das Problem der Demokratie*, 3rd ed., 1917). Seeking to show that democracy is the best regime type, he negates many of its essential characteristics, because he deems them—maybe if even rightfully so—to be disadvantageous. Of course, the opposite case is just as troubling. One cannot—as Hasbach does (*Die moderne Demokratie*, 1912)—consider constitutional monarchy to be the best form of state, if one wishes to provide an objective "political analysis" of democracy.

6. Rousseau, *Du contrat social*, Bk. I, Ch. 6. [Translation is Kelsen's own in "Foundations of Democracy," 21.]

7. Loc. cit., Bk. III, Ch. 15. [Translation is Kelsen's own in "Foundations of Democracy," 21.]

8. Contrary to appearances, common law also does not eliminate the contradiction between the social *ought* and the *is* of [the will of] the individual. It does, however, reduce that contradiction to a minimum by commanding to "conduct yourself as your fellows customarily tend to conduct themselves." Hence, the breach of law merely becomes the exception to the rule [*der Regel des Seins*]. Here, in contrast to the statute, common law evidences its democratic character, especially when the former—as was the case in times of old—appears in the form of a command issued by a deity, a priest, or a mythical king descended from the gods. Since its theory and practice became prominent precisely during periods of absolutism, common law tends to act as a contrarian principle and counterweight and, thus, to lead to the equalization of power [*Machtausgleich*].

9. Regarding the extent to which the here-described ideological transformation of liberalism or anarchism into a democratic étatism depends on the position held by the social groups espousing this ideology within the state and, in particular, on the relationship between the bourgeoisie and the proletariat, see my work *Allgemeine Staatslehre* (1925), p. 32f.

10. Rousseau's *volonté générale*—the anthropomorphic expression of the objective state order, whose validity is independent of the wills of individuals, i.e., of the *volonté* of the *tous*—is completely incompatible with the theory of a social contract, which is a function of the subjective *volonté* of the *tous*. However, this contradiction between a subjective and an objective construction, or—if one wishes—this movement from a subjective starting point to an objective end result, is no less characteristic of Rousseau as it is of Kant and Fichte.

11. Following Rousseau, loc. cit., Bk. IV, Ch. 2.

TWO

The People

The metamorphosis, which the idea of freedom undergoes, takes us from the idea of democracy to the reality of democracy, whose nature must be understood in terms of the antagonism, which is particularly characteristic for the problem of democracy, between ideology and reality. In arguments over democracy, a lot of misunderstanding is repeatedly created by the fact that one side only talks about the idea, while the other side only talks about the reality of this phenomenon. The two sides disagree because neither manages to capture the phenomenon in its entirety, where ideology and reality must be understood in reference to one another.[1] The importance of this antagonism between idea and reality is not limited to democracy's most basic principle, the idea of freedom, but it reveals itself in all of democracy's constituent elements. This is especially true for the concept of the People.

Theoretically, democracy is a political or social form in which the will of society or—less figuratively—the social order is generated by its subjects, the People. Democracy means that the leader and those who are led, that the Subject and Object of rule, are identical. It means the rule of the People over itself. Yet, what is "the People"? This idea, in which a multitude of individuals forms a unified entity, appears to be one of democracy's fundamental assumptions. The "People" as a unity is absolutely essential for democracy, since, theoretically at least, the former is not only—indeed not so much—the Object, as it is the Subject of rule.

Yet, from a concrete point of view, there is nothing more problematic than this unity which goes by the name, the People. Sociologically, it is riddled with national, religious, and economic differences and thus represents more a bundle of groups than a coherent, homogeneous mass.[2] Here, one can speak of unity only in a normative sense. As a consensus of thoughts, feelings, and wills and as a solidarity of interests, the unity of the People is an ethical-political postulate. National or state ideology asserts the reality of this postulate by way of a common, no longer questioned, fiction. At bottom, only a juristic fact is capable of circumscribing the unity of the People with some accuracy, namely: the unity of the state's legal order whose norms govern the behavior of its subjects.[3] A multiplicity of human actions is unified as the content of the norms making up the order. This unity, then, represents the "People" as an element of a particular social order, the state. As such a unity, the "People" is not, as is often naively imagined, a body or conglomeration as it were, of actual persons. Rather, it is merely a system of individual human acts regulated by the state legal order.

A person never belongs completely—that is with all of his or her functions and in all aspects of his or her spiritual and bodily being—to the social order, even if that order is the state (which, after all, tends to have the strongest hold on him or her).[4] This is most especially true with regard to a state whose form is based on the ideal of freedom. Invariably, the state order regulates only very specific aspects of an individual's life. A rather large part of human life must occur outside of that order and a certain sphere of human existence free from state interference must be retained. Therefore, it is a fiction when the unity, which the state legal order fashions out of the multiplicity of human actions, poses as a "popular body" by calling itself the "People." It creates the illusion that individuals belong to the People with their whole being, when in actuality they only belong to it through certain actions which are either commanded or prohibited by the political order. It is this illusion that Nietzsche tears down in his *Zarathustra* when he says of the "New Man": "State is the name of the coldest of all cold monsters. Coldly it tells lies too; and this lie crawls out of its mouth: 'I, the state, am the people.'"[5]

If the unity of the People must be understood as a unity of human acts normatively regulated by the legal order, then the People is unified only as an Object of rule in this normative sphere, where "rule" is defined as a normative bond or as the subjection to norms. Here, individuals are considered the Subject of rule only insofar as they participate in the creation of the state order. It is precisely in this function, when the "People" plays a role in government—a function which is so crucial for the idea of democracy—that the discrepancy between this definition of the "People" and its definition as a body of individuals subjected to norms comes to light. It is a self-evident fact that not all those who belong to the People as persons subjected to rule (that is, norms), can constitute the People as the ruling Subject as well, that is, participate in the norm-creating process, which is the decisive way that rule is exercised. It is so self-evident, in fact, that democratic ideologues are usually unaware of the gulf they are covering up when they identify the "People" in one sense with the "People" in the other sense.

Participation in government forms the content of so-called political rights. Even in a radical democracy, the People as an embodiment of those who hold political rights represents only a small segment of those beholden to the state order, i.e., of People as the Object of rule. Alone, certain natural considerations, such as age, mental health, and moral character, affect the extension of political rights and so represent barriers to the expansion of the "People" in its active sense—barriers, which do not, of course, apply to the "People" in its passive sense.

Quite revealing here is the fact that democratic ideology can tolerate the placement of even greater restrictions on [the concept of] the "People," where it embodies those who participate in rule. The exclusion of slaves and, to this day, of women does not preclude a political order from being described as democratic. Meanwhile, the privilege created by the institution of citizenship is treated as a matter of course, because it is assumed to be an essential feature of the state—a mistake, which derives directly from the aforementioned tendency to restrict political rights.[6]

Yet, the latest constitutional developments demonstrate that political rights do not necessarily have to be connected to citizenship. Breaking a thousand-year-old barrier, the constitution of Soviet Russia also grants all foreigners, who live in Russia for work-related reasons, full political equality. Given the exceedingly slow progress of the cosmopolitan idea [*Menschheitsgedankens*] in the theory of law, where those foreign to the state were at first considered downright outlaws and only gradually came to be granted civil—but, to this day, typically not political—equality, the Soviet constitution represents a step of historic proportions. Of course, an even greater regression has occurred in other respects (with the denial of political rights to certain categories of citizens in the name of class struggle).

In order to advance from the ideal to the real conception of the People, however, it is not enough merely to replace the mass of subjects with the much smaller group of individuals who possess political rights. One must go a step further and take into account the difference between the number of individuals who possess political rights and the number of individuals who actually exercise them—a difference that, though it varies according to the degree of political interest, is always quite considerable and can only be reduced through systematic education in democracy.

Since the "People," as the foundation for the democratic idea, is a ruling, and not a ruled, People, another restriction must be admitted from a realistic viewpoint. Among those who in fact exercise their political rights by participating in government, one would have to differentiate between the mindless masses who follow the lead of others and those few who—in accordance with the idea of democracy—decisively influence the governmental process based on independent judgment. Following this line of investigation, we encounter one of real democracy's most important elements: the political party, which brings like-minded individuals together in order to secure them actual influence in shaping public affairs.

These social organizations usually retain an amorphous character. They take the form of loose associations or, often, lack any legal form at all. Yet, a substantial part of the governmental process occurs within these parties: Like subterranean springs feeding a river, their impulses usually decisively influence the direction of the governmental process before it surfaces and is channeled into a common riverbed in the popular assembly or parliament.

Modern democracy virtually rests on political parties, whose importance grows the more the democratic principle is realized in practice. Under such circumstances, (admittedly still weak) attempts to anchor political parties constitutionally and to fashion them legally into what they factually already are—into organs of government—are certainly understandable. This tendency forms merely one part of a process, which has been aptly referred to as the "rationalization of power"[7] and goes hand in hand with the democratization of the modern state.

Resistance to this rationalization in general and to the definition of political parties as constitutional organs of the state in particular is not insubstantial, however. After all, it is not all that long ago that the existence of political parties was either ignored or openly rejected in the legislative and executive spheres of the state. Even today, there is not sufficient awareness about the fact that the hostility of the old monarchies toward parties and the ideological claim, particular to constitutional monarchies, that the political party and the state stand in contradiction to one another are nothing more than thinly disguised attacks on democracy.

It is a well-known fact that, because he is unable to achieve any appreciable influence on government, the isolated individual lacks any real political existence. Democracy is only feasible if, in order to influence the will of society, individuals integrate themselves into associations based on their various political goals. Collective bodies, which unite the common interests of their individual members as political parties,[8] must come to mediate between the individual and the state. Thus, there can be no serious doubt that efforts by constitutional monarchies to discredit political parties both theoretically and juristically constituted an ideologically veiled resistance to the realization of democracy. Only self-deception or hypocrisy could lead one to suppose that democracy is possible without political parties. A democratic state is necessarily and unavoidably a multiparty state.

This conclusion merely confirms what is already factually the case. Just a look at the development of democracies in history already disproves the thesis, widespread even today, that the political party and the state are essentially irreconcilable, and that the latter by its very nature cannot be based on a social structure like the former.[9] Political reality proves the opposite to be true. As is so often the case, what claims to be the "essence" or "nature" of the state here is really only a particular, namely antidemocratic, ideal.[10]

What, after all, is it that makes the political party appear to stand in essential contradiction to the state? It is said that the political party is merely an association of group interests and, thus, based on self-interest, while the state represents the common interest of all and, thus, stands above group interests and the political parties, which organize them.

First of all, it should be pointed out that besides interest-based parties, there are also ideological parties, which play an important role particularly within the German state. Admittedly, even these parties are not all too different from associations of interest. From a critical standpoint, which manages to see through the veil of ideology projected by every power apparatus, however, most states themselves historically prove to be nothing more than organizations, which disproportionately serve the interests of a ruling group.

At best, depicting the state as a tool for the common interests of a unified community confuses the *ought* with the *is*, the ideal with reality. As a rule, however, it is simply an attempt to idealize, or rather justify, reality for political reasons. Incidentally, the ideal notion of a common interest, which stands above and apart from group interests and, hence, "above partisanship," ["*überparteilich*"] proves to be a metaphysical—or, better, meta-political—illusion. This illusory idea of a solidarity of interests among all of society's parts—free from religious, ethnic, economic, and other differences—is commonly expressed in terms of an "organic" or "organically" arranged community, which is then contrasted with the so-called multiparty state and with mechanical democracy. Merely the answer to the question as to what other type of social grouping should replace the party as a factor in the governmental process shows just how dubious this entire argument against the political party is. For there is little choice but to assign the role parties play today to vocational groups. The self-interested character of these groups—whose political significance shall be investigated later—is not less, indeed may in fact be stronger, than that of political parties, since the former can only deal with economic interests.[11]

Conflicts of interest are an experiential and, here, unavoidable fact. Hence, if the will of society is not to be the expression of the interests of one group alone, that will must be the result of a compromise between opposing interests. The division of the People into political parties, in truth, establishes the organizational preconditions for the achievement of such compromises and the possibility of steering the will of society in a moderate direction. Consciously or not, a position, which opposes the formation of parties and so ultimately democracy itself, aids political forces that aim to achieve the sole domination of a single group's interest. To the extent that this interest is unwilling to tolerate opposition, it seeks to disguise itself ideologically as the "organic," "true," or "apparent" interest of all. In a democratic multiparty state, however, where the will of society emerges from competing parties, there is no need for the fiction of an "organic" common will.

The division of the People into political parties is an unavoidable development in all democracies. In fact, since the "People" does not actually exist as a viable political force prior to its organization into parties, it is more accurate to state that the development of democracy permits the integration of isolated individuals into political parties and, hence, first unleashes social forces that can be reasonably referred to as the "People." Thus, when democratic constitutions—which are still subject to the influence of monarchic ideology in this and many other points—deny political parties legal recognition, this no longer has the same meaning as it did under constitutional monarchies: Rather than seeking to hinder the realization of democracy, they are simply refusing to face facts.

Furthermore, anchoring political parties in the constitution provides the possibility for democratizing the aspects of the governmental process that occur within the parties' sphere of influence. This fact is all the more important, since it is presumably the amorphous structure of the parties that allows the political processes that occur within in them take on an explicitly aristocratic-autocratic character.[12] This is true even of parties pursuing a radically democratic program. Within the party, leading personalities are able to assert themselves much more forcefully than within the limits of a democratic state constitution. Party life is still governed by so-called party discipline, a serious equivalent of which does not exist in the interaction among parties—that is, in the sphere of parliamentary politics. Hence, the inner workings of the party offer the individual only a limited degree of democratic self-determination.

The transformation that leads from the ideal to the real conception of the "People" is therefore no less profound than the metamorphosis undergone by the idea of "freedom" in its movement from its natural to its political conception. Consequently, the existence of an extraordinary gulf not just between ideology and reality, but even between ideology and the maximum possibility of its realization, must be acknowledged. Rousseau's famous claim that there never has been nor ever will be a democracy in the true sense of the word, because the natural order of things—where the majority rules and the minority is ruled[13] —forbids it, must hence be understood as more than just rhetorical hyperbole.

While natural freedom and the ideal concept of the People have been reduced to political self-determination via majority rule and a much narrower circle of persons possessing and exercising political rights, respectively, we have by no means reached the end of the reductions, which the idea of democracy suffers in social reality. For only in a direct democracy is the social order in fact created by a majority of all persons possessing and exercising political rights in a popular assembly. Given the size and manifold responsibilities of the modern state, however, direct democracy no longer represents a feasible political form. Rather, modern democracy must be indirect; it must be a parliamentary democracy, in which the ruling will of society is created by a majority of those who are elected by the majority of persons possessing political rights. As a result, political rights—and therefore freedom—are essentially reduced to the right to vote. Of all previously mentioned limitations placed on the idea of freedom and, hence, the idea of democracy, parliamentarism may be the most significant. Thus, one must primarily understand parliamentarism, if one wishes to grasp the true nature of today's democracies.

NOTES

1. Regarding the ideology-reality dualism that characterizes all social bodies, see my paper in "Verhandlungen des Fünften Deutschen Soziologentages" (Tübingen, 1926), p. 38ff.

2. See my work *Der soziologische und der juristische Staatsbegriff*, 2nd ed. (1928), p. 4ff.

3. "From the standpoint of democracy, the will of the People does not exist as a tangible and unified entity. The People is comprised of the wills of many individuals. The majority of these wills becomes the will of the People, because the individuals enter into a legal, regular relationship to one another as law-abiding subjects. The fact that, next to the protection of the autonomy of each individual, there inheres in the creative force of law [*schöpferische Rechtskraft*] a particular will of society goes unnoticed by the ideologues of democracy" (Koigen, loc. cit., p. 142). This may suggest that the unity of the People is only possible in an organizational sense, that is, as a legal order. Hence, the question occasionally posed by Koigen: "Maybe the concepts of the People and of Law are identical?" (loc. cit., p. 7).

4. See my work *Allgemeine Staatslehre*, p. 149ff.

5. Nietzsche, *Also sprach Zarathustra*, pt. I. [The translation is based on Friedrich Nietzsche, *Thus Spoke Zarathustra: A Book for None and All*, trans. Walter Kaufmann (New York: Penguin Books, 1978), 48.]

6. See my work *Allgemeine Staatslehre*, p. 159ff.

7. See B. Mirkine-Guetzévich, "Die Rationalisierung der Macht im neuen Verfassungsrecht," in *Zeitschrift für öffentliches Recht* (VIII/2), p. 259ff.

8. Within a party, the individual disappears even more than within the state as a whole, whose order [after all] grants him subjective rights and, hence, the status of a legal subject. Alone this strong collectivizing tendency of the party shows that to view parties as the result of an "atomistic-individualistic theory of the state," as Triepel does in *Die Staatsverfassung und die politischen Parteien* (Berlin, 1927), p. 31, misjudges their very nature. Individualism is of course opposed to the party system, as Rousseau, for instance, argues and Triepel himself (loc. cit., p. 10) is forced to admit.

9. A typical representative of this dogma is Triepel, whose work cited above is largely dedicated to articulating this viewpoint. "Indeed," he says, "how could the legal order make government mainly and formally dependent upon the wills of social organizations, which in their being, scope, and character are the most unpredictable of all mass associations; which can come into being, disappear again, or change their principles suddenly; which only after a few decades may no longer retain any of their core principles except for their names;

and which in certain states are established according to completely incommensurable and, at times, politically entirely irrelevant principles."

That this characterization of political parties corresponds to the actual conditions in large democracies, such as the United States and England with their relatively permanent parties (the Democratic and Republican parties in the former and the Conservative, Liberal, and Labour parties in the latter), cannot seriously be contended. Triepel himself states that "the two-party system causes parties to ossify." But also in Germany, Austria, and even France, Triepel's depiction does not correspond to reality.

He then continues in his description of parties with the following: "which by their nature are based on self-interest and, therefore, already from the very start resist incorporation into the organic community of the state; which do not even always accept the state as such; and whose noblest activity is mutual conflict." We will have occasion to return to the idea of "self-interest" as the foundation of parties in a different context. Here, I only wish to note that if the "self-interested" nature of parties makes them unfit for incorporation into the community of the state, then not so much the existence of the party, but that of the state appears problematic; for the nature of the individuals, who are supposed to make up this community of the state, appears to be based not less, but apparently to an even higher degree on "self-interest." The self-interested nature of parties, however, can only derive from the individuals who comprise them. "Parties" that reject the state as such are hardly possible. Apart from its ideology, even a party espousing anarchism in reality aims like all other non-conservative parties for a [mere] re-organization of the state.

Triepel concludes: "in general the idea of a multiparty state is based on an almost irresolvable contradiction." He claims that it is the dominant opinion in Europe—and this is presumably the way in which Triepel views his own opinion—that the modern party system is "the symptom of a disease," a [sign of] "decay" (p. 29). It is hence essentially the same view, which—according to Triepel's own depiction—"the Germany citizen of the Biedermeier period" held. That citizen "viewed parties as a danger to the tranquility of the state; indeed, he was not disinclined to view the party system as a moral perversity" (p. 10). The reason for this [however] was not that the citizen of that period was, as Triepel believes, "no democrat, but a liberal"—for the liberals of that time were also democrats—but because the ideology of monarchy, which to a large extent had been perpetuated by legal science, had managed to exert its influence over this "citizen of the Biedermeier period"!

10. The desire to deduce—in order to defend a [particular] political postulate—from the nature of the state or the state's legal order that the political party is incompatible with these must obviously come into conflict with the reality of not just social conditions, but also of positive law and of the given state. Triepel asks a—what for him is a "fateful"—question: "Whether the modern, and especially the German, state has taken on the character of a multiparty state . . . i.e., of a state that integrates political parties so permanently into its organization, that the will and the actions of the state in decisive matters are dependent on the will and the actions of parties" (p. 7). This question is directed toward reality, whether in the sociological or in the juristic sense; his answer, however, is based on a (political) value [judgment], which does not correspond to reality. By proving that state and party stand in an essential contradiction to one another, Triepel wants to show that the modern state is no multiparty state, because the latter—according to Triepel's theory regarding the nature of the state and of the party—cannot exist in the first place! "In the legislative and executive spheres, in the matter of the "integration" of the state, which, after all, is ultimately the

only matter that concerns us, the party is an extra-constitutional phenomenon. Its decisions are, from a legal standpoint, the nonbinding and non-authoritative pronouncements of a social body foreign to the organism of the state. Thus, the claim that the modern state is 'built' upon parties turns out to be juristically untenable" (pp. 24, 25).

Yet, Triepel himself is forced to admit that "under the pressure of circumstances" the original hostility of the state legal order—which was the legal order of the monarchical state—toward parties has undergone a change (pp. 15–16). And he himself enumerates a plethora of positive legal rules, where the political party is posited as a factor in government and particularly in the electoral process. That this development would be incapable of going any further cannot seriously be contended. Deeming individual aspects of this development to be "strange" or "grotesque" (p. 22) are subjective value judgments. They cannot change the reality of positive law. What sense does it make, then, when Triepel categorically asserts that the party is an "extra-constitutional phenomenon"? After all, he even admits that, with regard to the efficacy of the party system, actual conditions have advanced much further than can be deduced from the legal orders [themselves] and these phenomena are "nothing arbitrary or coincidental," but rather the result of an "entirely natural process" (p. 27). Of course, this does not prevent him later from once again calling them "symptoms of disease" and "forms of degeneration." Indeed, he even states that "it would be a matter of burying one's head in the sand, if one sought to deny that the reality of political life does not entirely correspond with the picture painted by positive law. In deed and reality, the executive [*Regierung*] of the state is in fact at the mercy of political parties" (p. 26)—in order to confess finally "that even here (in Germany) the multiparty state has become a matter of fact" (p. 27). Is this the multiparty state, which according to Triepel is a "contradiction" in itself? Is it the one with regard to which he says that it is a "juristically untenable claim" to assert that the state rests upon parties, which he dismisses as "extra-constitutional" phenomena and as juristically nonexistent (pp. 24, 25)? Has Germany maybe ceased to be a "state" and the parties ceased to be parties, because Germany is a multiparty state?

Triepel has occasionally accused the pure theory of law, which I argue for, of formalism and sought to counter it with a constitutional legal theory "that is truer to life" and that strives "to place legal norms in an intimate relationship with the political forces that give rise to and shape [these norms] and that are in turn regulated by the law of the state [*vom staatlichen Rechte gemeistert werden*]" (*Staatsrecht und Politik*, 1926, pp. 17, 18). I fear that—at least with regard to the problem of the political party—Triepel's constitutional legal theory is mired in abstract formalism much more deeply than the pure theory of law. For the latter wishes to be a theory of positive law only and would certainly recognize that law as valid even if it takes on a content that the theoretician deems harmful. It is precisely for this reason that the theory strives for "purity"; it would rather suffer the—albeit undeserved and by Triepel not substantiated—charge of formalism than be accused of being only true to the "life" it finds politically amenable and of placing the legal norms of the state in an intimate relationship with the "political forces" it subjectively deems valuable.

Yet, this is the typical method employed by traditional constitutional legal theory! That which is deemed politically desirable is deduced from the nature or concept of the state, while that which is politically rejected is proven to contradict the nature or concept of the state. Is this not in fact the actual "conceptual jurisprudence" ["*Begriffsjurisprudenz*"]? Understandably, such a method must oppose the separation of law and politics. Only, [its practitioners] must not be surprised if their political opponents use the same method to prove the exact opposite.

11. Triepel, who rejects the political party as a constitutive element of the state because it is based upon "self-interest," believes that "vocational structures could serve as a foundation for the state" as long as "they are based upon such a simplicity and homogeneity of the interests of its members, that they do not contain any conflicts, which political parties could use as an opportunity to intervene in their affairs" (p. 30). The fact that political parties are based upon "self-interest" simply means that they are communities of interest. Hence, vocational groups are no different from political parties, for the former are merely communities of interest as well. Only when the community of interest, which they represent, is the more permanent one—and this is the [actual] meaning of Triepel's analysis—will vocational groups be a match for political parties.

In utterly rejecting the multiparty state—and this really means rejecting modern democracy—a jurist of Triepel's stature is obligated to explain what he wants to put in its place. Indeed, he does so: "The atomistic-individualistic conception of the state," which Triepel erroneously considers to be at the root of the party system, must be "given up and replaced by an organic conception." Now, what is to be the nature of this "organic" conception? The transition will only occur slowly. Yet, the final hour of the multiparty state will [eventually] strike. Already, other community-building forces are at work. "These [forces] will gradually lead via a natural development"—yet, according to Triepel, a "completely natural process" also brought about the multiparty state—"to a new organization of the People, which will be transformed from a soulless mass into a lively manifold unity [*Einheit in der Vielheit*]."

The notion that the People in a democracy—[though] Triepel only speaks of a multiparty state—constitutes a "soulless mass" does nothing to explain what the "organic" [form of organization] in the future state will look like; surely, "manifold unity" is also just another meaningless expression. Triepel reckons that "many will consider such a prediction a romantic illusion." Given that this "prediction" is entirely without content, there is surely little danger of that. Thus, based on what he has previously revealed about this newly emerging state, with which he obviously sympathizes, one can hardly make sense out of his assurance that "what is about to emerge as an organic form out of today's mechanized society is neither fairy tale nor apparition, but very real in nature." That democratic society is "mechanized" also does not answer the question of what the "organic" state will look like.

One is given nothing beyond the fact that it will be an "organism": "Once the forces struggling with elemental might to emerge from the bosom of the People, the forces of a new, territorially and personally diverse form of economic and intellectual self-administration"—"self-administration" is a rather democratic concept—"are successfully pressed into the service of the state, which they are meant not to destroy, but to hold together, and once the state is not dismantled, but, to the contrary, built from the bottom up, then the state will have become a true organism, where 'all weaves itself into the whole, each living in the other's soul.'" In the end, Triepel expresses the wish that he "may witness with my very own eyes that fair creature, which can appear to us today in thought only as a beautiful vision of the future" (p. 31). Apart from the aversion to democracy, his words, with all due respect, are without meaning.

Yet, the document is exceedingly characteristic of the "organic" conception of the state, which is offered in opposition to democracy.

12. This has been shown by Robert Michels in his work *Zur Soziologie des Parteiwesens*, 2nd ed.

13. Rousseau, loc. cit., Bk. III, Ch. 4.

THREE

Parliament

The battle, which was waged against autocracy at the end of the eighteenth and at the beginning of the nineteenth centuries, was essentially a battle for parliamentarism.[1] A constitution would give parliament decisive influence in government and put an end to the dictatorship of the absolute monarch and the privileges of the estates. Such a constitution, it was hoped, would lead to every imaginable form of political progress, the creation of a just social order, and the dawn of a new and better age. Indeed, as the defining political form of the nineteenth and twentieth centuries, parliamentarism can point to quite respectable achievements, including the complete emancipation of the bourgeoisie against the privileges of the aristocracy and, later, the political equality of the proletariat and, as a consequence, the beginning of its moral and economic emancipation against the propertied class.

Current historiography and the political ideology of today, however, do not judge parliamentarism favorably. Parties both on the extreme Right and on the extreme Left reject the parliamentary principle with an ever greater intensity and their calls for a dictatorship or a corporative[2] order are growing louder. Even among moderate parties, the fact that this erstwhile [parliamentary] ideal has undergone a certain chilling effect is undeniable. Let us not delude ourselves: Today people have gotten a little tired of parliamentarism, even though at this point one can hardly speak, as some authors have done, of a "crisis," a "bankruptcy," or even the "death throes" of this political form.

Of course, doubts about the merits of the parliamentary principle were already being expressed during the middle and end of the preceding century. Under the rule of a constitutional monarchy, however, such anti-parliamentary tendencies were, for quite understandable reasons, of little significance. In the face of a slowly, but unstoppably growing democratic movement based in parliament, these tendencies remained without effect.

It is a completely different matter, however, when parliamentarism is called into question at a time when that principle itself has achieved complete and absolute dominance, as is the case today. Within a parliamentary-democratic republic, the problem of parliamentarism constitutes a fateful question. The very existence of modern democracy depends on whether parliament proves to be a suitable tool for solving the social problems of our time. Democracy and parliamentarism are certainly not identical. Since direct democracy is impossible within the modern state, however, there can be little doubt that parliamentarism represents the only realistic form of government capable of putting the democratic ideal into practice under today's social conditions. Hence, the decision regarding parliamentarism is at the same time a decision regarding democracy.

The so-called crisis of parliamentarism was brought about not least by a critique that misinterprets the nature of this political form and thus misjudges its value. Alone, what is the nature of parliamentarism? Here, one should not confuse the objective nature with the subjective interpretation, which is offered up either consciously or unconsciously by those who participate or have a stake in the institution. Parliamentarism means government by a collegial organ democratically elected by the People based on universal, equal suffrage and the principle of the majority.

If one considers the ideas that define the parliamentary system, it becomes apparent that it is the idea of democratic self-determination, and so the idea of freedom, that predominates. The fight for parliamentarism was a fight for political freedom. This fact is easily forgotten by those who, often unfairly, criticize parliamentarism today. The possession of freedom, whose very existence only parliamentarism guarantees, has become so commonplace that it is no longer appreciated. This has led to the belief that freedom can be discarded as a political value. Yet, the idea of freedom is and remains the bedrock of all political speculation, even though—or maybe precisely because—this idea essentially negates everything social and political and, therefore, forms the counterpoint to all social theory and political practice. It is precisely for this reason that freedom cannot—as we have seen—exist in the social, let alone the political, sphere in its pure form, but is forced to amalgamate with certain alien elements.

Within the parliamentary principle, the idea of freedom thus once again emerges in a dual relationship, which constrains that idea's original force. First, it is linked with the majority principle, whose connection with the idea of freedom has already been investigated and to whose real function within the parliamentary system we will return later. The second element, which an analysis of parliamentarism brings to light, however, is the indirect nature of this form of government. In other words, we encounter the fact that the will of the state is not directly produced by the People itself, but by a parliament chosen by the People.

Here, freedom—as self-determination—allies itself with the essential desire for a division of labor and social differentiation. Here, it joins with a tendency that contradicts the basic, primitive character of the democratic idea of freedom, which by itself stipulates that the will of the state in all of its manifold manifestations be determined directly by one and the same assembly of all citizens entitled to vote. Every differentiation within the state organism based on the division of labor, and the assignment of any state function to an organ other than the People, necessarily entails the restriction of freedom. Parliamentarism thus represents a compromise between the democratic demand for freedom and the division of labor, which is the necessary basis for all progress in social technique.

Attempts have been made, however, to cover up the not insubstantial injury, which the idea of democracy suffers as a result of the fact that it is not the People that governs, but rather a parliament, which—though elected—is an organ quite different from the People. On the one hand, one could not seriously accept a primitive form of direct democracy, since the complexity of social conditions made the advantages of labor division indispensable. The larger the political community, the less the "People" as such is able to engage directly in the truly creative aspects of government. Here, alone for purely social-technical reasons, the People must limit itself to the creation and control of the actual governing apparatus.

On the other hand, there was a desire to create the illusion that even in a parliamentary system the idea of democratic freedom, and only this idea, would be given unimpaired expression. This was [and is] achieved through the fiction of representation, according to which parliament is only a proxy for the People, and that the People can only express its will in and through parliament. This fiction is maintained even though the parliamentary principle in all constitutions is invariably linked with a rule barring representatives from taking binding instructions from their constituents, thus making parliament legally independent of the People.[3] Indeed, it is with this declaration of independence from the People that the modern parliament comes into being in the first place, since it clearly differentiates this organ from the old estate assembly, whose members were bound by and responsible to the mandates of their constituent groups.

The fiction of representation is meant to legitimate parliamentarism from the standpoint of popular sovereignty. Yet, this obvious fiction, which is designed to cover up the real and fundamental injury suffered by the principle of freedom at the hands of parliamentarism, has played into the hands of the opposition by providing it with the argument that democracy is based on a palpable lie. Nevertheless, though the fiction of representation has been unable to fulfill its actual purpose of justifying parliament from the standpoint of popular sovereignty, it has served a function quite different from the one for which it was originally intended: It has managed to keep the nineteenth- and twentieth-century political movement standing under enormous pressure from the democratic ideal on a sensible and moderate path. By creating the belief that the popular masses politically determine themselves through the elected parliament, this fiction has prevented excessive overburdening of the democratic idea in political practice. Such overburdening could have endangered social progress, since it would have necessarily been accompanied by an unnatural primitivization of political technique.

Understandably, the fictitious nature of the idea of representation did not move to the forefront of political consciousness as long as democracy was still engaged in a battle against autocracy, and parliamentarism itself had not yet entirely prevailed against the pretensions of the monarch and of the estates. Under a constitutional monarchy, where a popularly elected parliament had to be viewed as the maximum possibility of what could be politically wrested from the formerly absolute monarch, it made little sense to offer a critique based on whether this political form is actually capable of fully representing the will of the People.

This changed, however, as soon as the parliamentary principle—particularly within the republic—had achieved complete victory. When parliamentary rule with its appeal to the principle of popular sovereignty replaced constitutional monarchy, the glaring fiction inherent in the theory already articulated in the French Assembly of 1789—that parliament by its very nature is nothing more than a representative of the People, whose will alone is given expression in parliamentary acts—could no longer escape criticism. Little wonder then that the leading argument against parliamentarism today rests upon the revelation that the will of the state articulated by parliament is not the will of the People, and that, in fact, parliament cannot express the People's will, because the constitutions of parliamentary states do not allow—except in the case of parliamentary elections—for the articulation of such a will.

This argument is correct; it is only effective, however, so long as one attempts to legitimize parliamentarism based on the principle of popular sovereignty and believes that the nature of parliamentarism can be derived entirely from the idea of freedom. Then, of course, parliamentarism has promised to do something, which it has not been and will never be able to do. Yet, as has been shown at the beginning, it is possible to define the nature of parliamentarism without recourse to the fiction of representation and, instead, to justify its value as a specific social-technical means for the creation of the state order.

If parliamentarism is understood as a necessary compromise between the primitive idea of political freedom and the principle of the division of labor, then one is already able to discern clearly the direction that a possible reform of parliamentarism has to take. Still, one may first want to consider whether the complete elimination of parliamentarism is even politically feasible today; that is, we need to investigate what chances of success the removal of parliament from the organization of the modern state has in the first place. It is certainly no coincidence, but reflective of a law governing the structural development of social bodies, that something like a parliament exists in every reasonably technically advanced polity. Particularly noteworthy is the fact that even in extreme autocracies, the monarch is compelled to call on the support of a group of men, who stand at his side as an advisory council (or under some similar appellation) and who prove especially useful for the preparation, deliberation, and assessment of general orders and norms issued in his name. If, in a larger polity, the People as a whole is unable to govern in an unmediated fashion, then the same thing is also true for the single autocrat, and this in part for the same reasons: a lack of knowledge and ability and an aversion to responsibility.

The fact that the members of the assembly are chosen by the autocrat in the one case and elected by the People in the other is surely a matter of importance. Still, it is important more from an ideological standpoint than from the standpoint of social reality, that is, with regard to the real functions this organ performs. Certainly, whether the organ is given an advisory function or the power of decision is also significant. Even here, however, an analysis that is directed at actual relations and psychological efficacy, rather than at juristic form, will sometimes be unable to discover any great difference between the parliament in a democracy and the advisory council of the absolute monarch. This is particularly true if one takes into account that, even in a modern democracy, a very significant, if not outwardly visible, part of the legislative work does not actually occur within the parliamentary process, but rather within the executive.[4] The executive must have the power of direct and indirect initiative in a parliamentary democracy no less than it does in a constitutional monarchy. On the other hand, the authority of those assembled in a council very often provides them with much greater influence vis-à-vis the monarch than is apparent from the constitution alone.

In a technically advanced social body, the fact that the executive organ (and its subordinate bureaucratic apparatus) is accompanied by a special, namely collegial, legislative organ seems to be a necessary social development. This necessity seems to have its source not least in the very nature of the process by which the will of the state is created. Given that psychologically speaking there are only individual human wills, it is presupposed here that the phenomenon, which is commonly referred to as the figurative "will" of society in general and of the state in particular, does not constitute a real, psychological fact.[5] The so-called will of the state is simply the anthropomorphic expression for the ideal social order, which claims to embody the plethora of individual human acts that occur within it. As the embodiment of such acts, the social order is a complex of norms and "ought"-regulations, which govern the behavior of the people belonging to the society and in this way first constitute the society as such.

The demand that the members of society behave a certain way lies at the heart of the social order. This demand is expressed most vividly, and so most comprehensibly for the great masses to whom it is addressed, with the words: the community or the state—hypostatized as a person—"wills"—as if it were human or superhuman—that its members behave a certain way. The "ought" of the state order is imagined to be the "will" of a personified state. Consequently, the "creation of the will of the state" is nothing else but the process of producing the state order.

An essential feature of this process is that it is transformed via a number of intermediate steps from an initially abstract form into a concrete one, i.e., from a complex of general norms into individual acts of state. Unlike the development of the psychological will in humans, it is a process of concretization and individuation, within which two completely dissimilar functions or stages are clearly differentiated: the creation of general, abstract norms, on the one hand, and the enactment of concrete individual decrees, orders, and decisions on the other.

It belongs to juridical phenomenology to describe the difference between these functions.[6] Even in thoroughly primitive social groups, one can verify the existence of these two functions or stages in the creation of the will of society. Admittedly, the impetus to create a special organ for the creation of general norms exists only when this stage is elevated from an unconscious, habitual exercise on the part of the subjects to a process of conscious articulation. Yet, only a very superficial viewpoint narrowly limited to the most primitive groups could suppose that the will of society, which constitutes the social group, could directly and exclusively be expressed in the form of individual commands and individual coercive acts. Such a viewpoint fails to recognize that a general normative order—internalized, if only unconsciously, by all or at least certain members of the group—is required for the organs that issue the social commands to function. The governing organs in a primitive group are even less capable of freely enacting decisions and decrees without being bound to general norms than those in a modern state. Precisely the former feel themselves bound to general norms to a very high degree; and those norms have an even greater influence insofar as they tend to have a religious or magical character. More than through individual social commands, the community comes alive in the consciousness of its members through the general norms governing their mutual behavior. The function of creating general norms, however, will always tend to lead to the creation of a collegial, and not a unitary, organ.

Consequently, attempts to eliminate parliament from the organism of the modern state are unlikely to be successful in the long run. At bottom, only the way in which parliament is appointed and composed and the extent of its competency can come into question. In the end, even efforts striving for a corporative organization of the state or for a dictatorship amount to a mere reform of parliamentarism, regardless of how much their programs postulate the latter's destruction.[7]

NOTES

1. In regard to what follows, see my work *Das Problem des Parlamentarismus* (1925) and the literature cited there.

2. [The German adjective *berufständisch* can be translated several ways. I have generally translated it as "corporative," which I believe conveys most accurately the historical meaning of the term as Kelsen uses it here, though occasionally I have also translated it as "vocational" or "professional" where such deviation was appropriate (particularly with reference to "vocational groups").]

3. Regarding the fiction of representation, see my *Allgemeine Staatslehre*, p. 310ff.

4. [As I have used "government" to translate *Gesellschafts-* and *Staatswillensbildung*, I am adopting the American translation "executive" for *Regierung*.]

5. See my *Hauptprobleme der Staatsrechtslehre*, 2nd ed. (1925), p. 97ff., and *Allgemeine Staatslehre*, p. 65ff.

6. See Merkl, *Allgemeines Verwaltungsrecht* (1928), pp. 85, 157ff.

7. Karl Marx comments that the Paris Commune of 1871 should not have been a parliamentary body, but a working body [*arbeitende Körperschaft*], and that universal suffrage, instead of merely being a matter of deciding once every three or six years what member of the ruling class should represent, or oppress, the People in parliament, should in fact enable the People to intervene directly in the administrative sphere (*Bürgerkrieg in Frankreich*, 3rd ed., p. 47). Building on this observation, Lenin has in his writings, which are a seminal contribution to neo-communist theory, called for the abolition of parliament (*Staat und Revolution*, 1918, p. 40ff.). With this he believed he had struck a blow against true democracy [itself]; yet he did not even strike parliamentarism. On the point in question, the representative system established by the Bolsheviks in the Soviet constitution—for practical reasons, they of course could not and did not want to abandon representation altogether—not only fails to overcome democracy, but instead represents a return to it. The short terms of office, the possibility of recalling the People's delegates in the various soviets at a moment's notice and the resulting absolute dependence on the voters, the intimate contact with the primal will of the People—this is democracy in its truest form. The demand for a constant and lively relationship between popular representatives and their constituents already presupposes the latter's continual coordinated activity [*ständig beisammen seien*], so they can effectively exercise control over their delegates. Periodic meetings of the voters would not be able to fulfill this purpose.

If, however, each individual economic workplace —the factory, the workshop, the regiment—becomes an electoral body, in which those entitled to vote, because they are assembled in working communities, are in closest contact with one another on a daily basis; if each individual place of work votes in the local soviet, the local soviets vote in the provincial soviets, and these vote in the highest parliament for an all-Russian Congress of workers', farmers', and soldiers' councils, whose legislative and executive functions are in turn transferred to a 200-member central executive committee; then this not only furnishes the possibility of a permanent will of the People, but also the best possible guarantee that this will of the People is constituted not according to the arbitrariness of a voters' meeting, but according to the immanent logic that arises—if it does so at all—out of the continual and highly intimate contact that exists within the community of the workplace. Yet, when workers participate in or even take over the management of each individual economic workplace, it represents nothing other than the democratization of the economy. The feasibility or practicality of such a democratization is beyond the scope of this discussion. Here, the only intention is to highlight the fact that, with this demand, socialism is merely making use of a principle of democratic organization.

The democratic nature of the electorate's organization according to workplace, which is so characteristic of the Soviet constitution, may not—as the history of that constitution shows—have been initially intended. Yet, most social institutions attain in the course of their development a different meaning than was originally associated with them. Furthermore, this principle of [democratic] organization is by no means—nor can it be—carried out fully. Even if only those who work are entitled to vote—as it is the case in the Soviet constitution—there nonetheless are many workers who do not belong to a [fixed] workplace. These include intellectuals and small handworkers, but most of all peasant farmers. Hence, a constitution based on councils must, on the one hand, draw on alternate organizations such as labor unions, and, on the other hand, forgo completely an organization according to workplace with regard to workers in agriculture. Here, a purely territorial unit, the village, serves as the foundation for the electoral system. This admixture of organizational systems of course creates various disadvantages, about which we shall not go into further detail here. Similarly, we will not deal with the more important question of whether the politicization of the economic production process, which results from the use of the workplace as a permanent electoral body, does not endanger that process. Experiences in Russia confirm these fears only all too well. Yet, precisely this deficiency is exceedingly characteristic of direct democracy, which after all was only possible in the classical city-states because those who possessed political rights and those who did the work—namely, slaves—constituted fundamentally separate groups.

Given the impracticality of implementing direct democracy in large, economically and culturally advanced states, efforts to establish the most permanent and closest connection possible between the will of the People and popular representatives, whose existence is unavoidable, and the tendency toward at least an approximate form of immediacy do not lead to the elimination or even just the curbing of parliamentarism. Rather, they lead in a certain sense to the exact opposite, an unforeseen hypertrophy of parliamentarism. The Soviet constitution of Russia, which consciously and intentionally opposes the representative democracy of the bourgeoisie, clearly demonstrates this. The single parliament elected through general popular elections is replaced by a whole system of countless parliaments, which are based upon a pyramidal structure, known as "soviets" or councils, and merely function as representative bodies.

This extensification of parliamentarism goes hand in hand with its intensification. In neo-communism, parliaments are to be transformed from mere "prattle shops" [*Schwatzbuden*] into real working bodies. This, however, means: they should not limit themselves to the making of [general] law, to the establishment of general norms and common principles, but also take over the functions of the executive [*Executive*] and carry out the lawmaking process down to its final stage of concretization, to individual acts of state and to specific legal transactions. Indeed, it is because of this tendency that from the highest central parliament within that parliament's territorial and technical sphere of influence there radiate outward smaller local and specialized parliaments down to the individual workshop. Here, we have nothing other than an attempt to democratize not only the legislative, but also the administrative sphere. The bureaucratically, that is, autocratically, appointed official who within the quite expansive limits of the law had been authorized to impose his will upon a heretofore governed subject is now replaced by the latter. The Object of administration becomes its Subject. He does not do so directly, however, but through elected representatives. The democratization of the executive is at first merely a parliamentarization. See, in this regard, my work *Sozialismus und Staat*, 2nd ed. (1923).

Fascism too was initially marked by a passionate struggle against democracy and parliamentarism. Today, it invokes its plebiscitary—that is, no doubt, its directly and radically democratic—character and so far has by no means abolished parliament, but rather modified electoral laws in order to secure its party the majority in that body. See, in this regard, Robert Michels, *Sozialismus und Faszismus in Italien* (1925), p. 298ff. On p. 301, Michels points to the fact that fascism relies in its anti-parliamentarian tendencies on Vilfredo Pareto. The latter's "Political Testament" ("Testamento politico: Pochi punti d'un futuro ordinamento costituzionale," in *Giornale Economico*, I/18) states [according to Michels]:

> that to govern [*zur Regierung*] requires the consent of the masses, but not their participation. A reliance on a parliamentary majority is insufficient, because any majority is constantly in danger of fragmenting or falling apart. Yet, ruling by naked force is not advisable either. Governance [*Regierung*] must be rooted not merely in power, but also in the approval of public opinion. It is to this end that parliament and referendum generally prove quite useful. As a result, not even Pareto is inclined to advocate the abolition of parliament. The institution of popular representation exists and must therefore, he believes, be retained. The task of the statesman is entirely limited to devising to the best of his abilities ways and means of guarding against the danger posed by parliamentarism.

But what are the means Pareto suggests? Referendum and freedom of the press. These are radically democratic elements. When this anti-democratic and anti-parliamentarian theory with its aristocratic pretensions is compelled to make practical political proposals, it ultimately ends up at exactly the same point as the theory it is fighting. According to Michels's account on p. 302, Pareto contends that "the rule of the People does not count for much, but it always counts for more than the rule of popular representatives. Thus, the task at hand is to retain parliamentarism as a decorative element out of deference to the democratic ideologies still held by the People, but to render it harmless at the same time." This contention is not—as Michels argues—Machiavellian, but simply insincere; for this political theory does not in fact offer any better form of state than a parliamentarism limited by referendum. The fact that this form of state is regarded as an evil, even if as a relatively least evil, apparently has to do with the thoroughly liberal basic attitude, which is characteristic of Pareto.

FOUR

Reforming Parliamentarism

A reform of parliamentarism could move in the direction of once again strengthening its democratic element. For social-technical reasons, it is impossible to leave the creation of the state order at all of its levels to direct popular control. Nevertheless, a greater degree of participation by the People than is now the case is still possible within the parliamentary system, where popular participation currently remains limited to the act of voting. Undeniably, many a question might have been resolved differently, if not just parliament, but also the electorate itself had had a say. Whether such an appeal to the People would also lead to an [substantive] improvement in the governmental process is beyond the scope of this discussion. But faced with the argument of elitism [*Volksfremdheit*], which is often directed against parliamentarism, it should be pointed out that, even if the parliamentary principle is generally maintained, the institution of the referendum is capable and in need of further development.

It would clearly be in the interest of the parliamentary principle itself, if career politicians, who happen to be parliamentarians today, managed to repress their understandable aversion to the referendum. They should not just permit—as has already happened in several modern constitutions—the so-called constitutional referendum, but also an, if not obligatory, then at least facultative, referendum on laws. In that regard, experience shows that not already promulgated and standing laws but acts of parliament should be subject to a vote by the People. Conditions under which referenda have already proven useful are a conflict between the two parliamentary chambers and a motion by either the head of state or a qualified minority in parliament. If the ever increasing desire for the most direct popular influence possible in government is to be taken fully into account, then a conflict between [the results of] a referendum and a parliamentary act must lead to the dissolution of parliament and the election of a new parliamentary body. That new body may still not give direct expression to the will of the People, but at least it has not directly contradicted that will either.

Another institution that makes possible a certain degree of direct popular ingerence in government, while basically maintaining parliamentarism, is the petition: A certain minimum number of citizens, who are entitled to vote, can propose a bill, which must then be officially considered by parliament. This institution too should be expanded further than is currently the case in older as well as newer constitutions. In the process, the implementation of popular demands should be technically facilitated by not requiring the petition to present an already fully drafted bill, but only to offer general directives. If the electorate is not allowed to give binding instructions to its representatives in parliament, then it should at least have the opportunity to voice general suggestions, according to which parliament can then direct its legislative activities.

To be sure, the imperative mandate cannot return in its old form.[1] Yet, to a certain degree, the undeniable tendencies, which push in such a direction today, could be given forms that are compatible with the structure of the modern political apparatus. The introduction of proportional representation alone has necessitated a stricter degree of party organization than was needed with the simple majority system. As a result, the idea of a permanent control over the representative by the political party into which his constituents are organized cannot simply be dismissed today. The legal-technical possibility for the implementations of this kind of control certainly exists.

In addition, a legal guarantee for the constant, close contact between representatives and constituents could help reconcile the broad masses with the parliamentary principle. The lack of accountability of the representative towards his constituents is without a doubt one of the central causes of the ill-feeling that exists towards the institution of parliament today. Yet, contrary to the claims of nineteenth-century legal doctrine, this lack of accountability is by no means an essential element of the parliamentary system. And so, even in the constitutions of today there can be found certain beginnings, which deserve notice and are capable of further development.

First, however, one would have to eliminate or at least reduce the lack of accountability of the representative not toward voters, but toward state authorities and especially the courts. This lack of accountability, commonly referred to as [legislative] immunity, has long been an integral component of the parliamentary system. The privilege, that a representative can be pursued and arrested for a criminal act by the courts only with parliamentary approval, arose during the period of semi-feudal monarchy and so at a time when the conflict between parliament and the monarchical executive was most acute. The privilege may still have been justified within a constitutional monarchy, where this tension between parliament and the executive continued to exist, though in a different sense than before. Though significantly diminished by the independence of the judiciary, the danger of a representative being removed from parliament through an abuse of power by the executive had not yet been completely eliminated.

Within a parliamentary republic, however, where the executive is nothing more than an extension of parliament and is subject to the strictest control by the political opposition, indeed the entire public, and judicial independence is no less guaranteed than under a constitutional monarchy, it makes little sense to want to protect parliament from its own executive. Nor can the privilege in question be seriously characterized as a protection of the minority against the arbitrary will of the majority—a redefinition applied in democratic republics to some of the institutions that had been adopted from constitutional monarchies. This is true not least because such a protection from the majority remains impossible as long as that majority has the power to deliver representatives to the authorities pursuing them.

In no way does there any longer exist a legitimate claim to protection from prosecution, especially when one considers that the privilege of immunity is practically nothing else but an entirely unjustified debasement of the judicial protection afforded against slanderous attacks by other representatives. The practice of merely using parliamentary disciplinary procedures, such as the call to order, to punish criminal offences that are revealed by a representative in the course of a parliamentary speech—because they supposedly occurred in the exercise of office—is untenable today. If, during its long period of existence, parliamentarism has not only not secured the sympathies of the broad masses, but even less those of intellectuals, then this is not least due to the abuse engendered by the completely outmoded privilege of immunity.

With regard to the lack of accountability of representatives towards their voters, however, it is already a breakthrough when some newer constitutions stipulate that a representative, though he is not bound to the instructions of his constituents, nonetheless loses his mandate once he leaves or is expelled from the party for or by which he was elected. Such a stipulation arises naturally where voting occurs by party lists. For if the voter—as in this case—no longer exercises any influence over the selection of the candidates, and his vote is based solely on his allegiance to a particular party, then the candidate running for office—from the voter's standpoint—receives his mandate only on the basis of his membership in that party. Here, it is only logical that the representative must lose his mandate, if he no longer belongs to the party that sent him to parliament. But this presupposes the relatively permanent organization of voters into parties. Where political parties are formed merely for the purposes of an election, only to fall apart again afterwards, one cannot stipulate that a representative's retention of his mandate should be dependent upon his continuing membership in the particular party for or by which he was elected.

Since it can be unclear in some cases whether someone still belongs to a particular party—has a representative, for instance, permanently defected from his party if he occasionally voted against that party's intentions?—it is advisable that the loss of a mandate result only from an explicit resignation or expulsion from the party. Certain difficulties arise not so much over who should be able to decide about the existence of these conditions and, therefore, the loss of the mandate—for this, without a doubt, is best done by an independent and objective court. Rather, the problem lies more in deciding who should be entitled to apply for the initiation of such proceedings. Giving this power to the representative body itself runs the risk of never having such applications made in cases where the defection, which is threatened with the loss of a mandate, occurred in the interest of the majority or even helped create a new majority. Here, the party whose interests were endangered by the defection should actually be given the right to make the application.

The Soviet constitution of Russia goes much further. According to its provisions, members of the various councils can be recalled by their constituents at any time. It is particularly this aspect that has secured the Soviet constitution a great deal of sympathy from the working class in other countries. If one could be brought to organize political parties by law and, in fully implementing the idea of proportional representation, leave to each party the selection of the representatives to which it is numerically entitled, then nothing would stand in the way of giving the parties, which have now become integral elements of the constitution, also the right of recalling those representatives. Indeed, then one could begin to move toward the idea of not forcing political parties to send a fixed number of individually selected representatives to parliament, where these—and thus always the same—representatives must participate in deciding all questions, no matter how factually diverse those questions are. Instead, a political party could be left to delegate for the deliberation and passage of various laws experts from their midst, whose influence on [parliamentary] decisions would be proportional to the number of votes to which their respective party is entitled.[2]

This type of reform would help counter a recent argument that, next to the argument of elitism, is made most often against parliamentarism. Because of their very composition, parliaments are accused of lacking the expertise necessary for making sound laws for the differing domains of public life. While the claim that parliament is falsely passing off its will for the will of the People constitutes an appeal to the idea of freedom, which is not, at least sufficiently, realized by parliamentarism, the argument about a lack of parliamentary expertise aims in the opposite direction; namely, it aims toward the division of labor.

Accordingly, there exists, in line with the principle of labor division, a desire to replace the central and universal legislative organ with "technical parliaments" [*Fachparlamente*] in the various areas of legislative activity, since the former body, which is democratically elected, lacks any specific technical qualifications. The beginnings of these kinds of technical bodies, which would perhaps adjoin themselves to the departmental divisions of the administrative bureaucracy, can already be seen in the existence of specialized parliamentary committees. Since these committees handle all of the decisive legislative work, they already have reduced the plenum to a merely formal voting apparatus. Insofar as the technical parliaments—which cannot render a general, political parliament superfluous as a collective organ—are not chosen in general elections, but rather emanate from professionally, that is, corporatively, organized constituent groups, the demand for such bodies must by no means be interpreted as a call for the abolition of democracy in general and of parliamentarism in particular. Rather, it must be viewed as a reform of these toward a corporative organization of the governmental process.

In particular, it is the idea of a "corporative parliament" [*Wirt schaftsparlament*] that most recently strives for realization. For now, of course, it is meant as an additional advisory body of experts, possibly vested with a suspensory veto, next to the old parliament. The composition of this corporative parliament is meant to balance the numerous contradictions that exist within the production process, such as between agriculture and industry or manufacture and commerce, but also between producers and consumers, as well as employers and workers. The idea of entrusting government both to a general political parliament built upon the principle of democracy and to a corporatively organized representative body, with each of these chambers fundamentally equal to the other, is problematic in more than one respect. Since a clear separation of the "political" from the "economic" is impossible in most matters, as most economic matters have political, and most political matters have economic, relevance, the more important issues could only be settled via an agreement of both chambers. What sense there is in forming a bicameral legislative organ, where each of the constituent organs is based upon entirely different principles, remains a mystery. The reaching of an agreement between two chambers thusly constructed can more or less only be a matter of coincidence.

NOTES

1. The way in which political value judgments influence theory is shown clearly by the positions taken by Steffen and Hasbach on direct democracy and particularly on the imperative mandate. Steffen, for whom democracy is the best form of state, declares the imperative mandate to be undemocratic (Steffen, loc. cit., p. 93) because he deems it to be disadvantageous. Hasbach, who also perceives the imperative mandate as harmful but whose political ideal is the opposite of democracy, is quick to declare such a mandate to be a consequence [of the idea] of popular sovereignty (Hasbach, loc. cit., p. 322). On this point, the nature of democracy has actually been captured more accurately by its opponent.

2. See R. M. Delannoy, "Von der gebundenen Liste zur reinen Parteiwahl," in *Der österreichische Volkswirt* (17/34), p. 930ff.

FIVE

Corporative Representation

Meanwhile, many conservatives go beyond mere reform and demand that democratic parliamentarism be replaced completely by corporativism. In place of a "mechanical" there is to be an "organic" social arrangement. Instead of relying on the arbitrary will of the majority, every—vocationally organized—social group is to be given a share in government in accordance with its significance within the overall social structure.[1]

A closer look at corporativism, which many want to put in the place of a supposedly outdated parliamentarism, reveals that the realization of this idea faces extraordinary, partly insurmountable, difficulties. Chiefly, one cannot ignore the fact that a social arrangement according to vocation, which essentially is an arrangement according to shared interests, fails to capture all of the interests that are relevant to the governmental process. Vocational interests compete with other, entirely different and often vital, interests (religious, broadly ethical, and aesthetic concerns, for example). Just because someone is a farmer or a lawyer does not mean that he or she is only interested in agricultural or legal questions. What shape marriage law and the relation between church and state take are also matters of concern; and, in the end, everyone has an interest in a just, practicable, or even merely tolerable social order. Within what vocational group could all of these vital questions be decided?

Additionally, there is the oft-cited fact that a corporative arrangement has an immanent, natural tendency toward the most extensive differentiation, since the corporative idea is satisfied only when vocational groups are based on a complete commonality of interest. At an advanced economic and technological level, the number of different vocations entitled to their own independent organizations would necessarily go into the hundreds or even thousands. Even then, however, the demarcation between individual vocations would be more or less artificial.

Among the various vocational groups, however, the natural relationship is not one of a commonality, but of a conflict of interest; and it is precisely by the organization of common interests into individual vocational groups that this conflict is exacerbated. Yet, how are the manifold conflicts of interest among groups supposed to be decided? Certainly, purely occupational questions may find satisfactory solutions relatively easily when left to the autonomy of individual vocational groups; though it remains debatable whether the easier agreement between employers and employees within the same vocational group, which is often boasted about, is not principally due to the fact that here the economically weaker side is deprived of the support of its comrades in other groups. Still, many, maybe even most, questions cannot be regarded as purely internal and only touching upon the interests of the members of one group. Rather, other groups will also have an interest in how these questions are decided, and this often in a different sense than the group immediately involved. Yet, it is the resolution of these conflicts that is decisive. The ideology of corporativism itself does not provide an answer to this fundamental question.

Here, the only possible solution is to give the final decision over conflicts of interest between vocational groups to an authority, which is constituted according to non-corporative principles. This would have to be either a democratically elected parliament, whose members are drawn from the general population, or a more or less autocratically structured organ. Corporativism has no integrative principle of its own to counter the powerful tendency toward greater differentiation inherent in it. It has been rightly pointed out that, insofar one is not dealing with purely internal matters which can be left to the autonomy of the vocational groups, the ruling principle upon which the governmental process rests in a corporative constitution would have to be one of unanimous agreement among all the groups or at least of those who have a stake in the decision. This, of course, is practically impossible. Precisely this fact reveals how completely empty and useless the formula is, which the corporative idea usually offers in opposition to parliamentarism: that each group should be given a share in government according to its relevance to the whole. First of all: this corporative idea could not—as it is sometimes claimed—do away with the system of representation and, thus, with parliamentarism, but merely replace its democratic form with a different form of representation. The difference would consist solely in the fact that, unlike in a democracy where political parties—be it directly or indirectly—act as electoral bodies, this function would instead be fulfilled by vocational groups. For an unmediated form of government remains impractical even within the corporatively organized group. Thus, [the argument for a corporative form of representation] merely comes down to the realization of a "corporative parliament" [*Ständeparlament*].

Then, however, it must above all be clear who is to decide on the degree of importance that is given to each vocational group, who determines each group's position in the hierarchy, and what criteria should be followed in the process. Even if these—in fact, irresolvable—questions were resolved, and even if a corporative representative body representing the various vocational groups in proportion to their importance were established, there would still remain the question upon what basic principle a unified will could be achieved within such a representative body. Would one not, in the end, still have to depend on the "mechanical" principle of the majority? And if this were the case, would it still make sense to create such a representative body on the basis of corporative principles? For with either full or partial majority rule, it is more sensible to conduct the selection of parliamentary members based upon the premise that each voter is not just a member of a particular vocation, but a member of the state as a whole—thus, presuming that he or she is not just interested in occupational issues, but in all issues which may fall within the purview of the state. This, in the end, is the reason why corporativism can never completely replace the democratic parliament, but can only exist as an additional advisory organ next to the latter—or, instead, next to a monarch. Its primary function must always remain limited to giving clear expression to the interests involved in the legislative process, i.e., to inform the actual lawmaker. This is precisely why the idea of corporativism is insufficient for solving the problem of regime type. The decisive choice—democracy or autocracy—remains the same.

Given this state of affairs, it is no wonder that corporativism, insofar as it has been historically realized, has always remained a form in which one or more groups have sought to rule over the rest. Thus, one is not totally unjustified in suspecting that the recently renewed demand for the introduction of a corporative form of organization does not really express a desire for the organic—that is to say, just—participation of all vocational groups in government. Rather, it more likely reflects a struggle for power by certain interests, to whom a democratic constitution no longer seems to offer much hope for political success. Is it not strange that calls for corporativism are raised by the bourgeoisie at precisely the moment when the proletariat, which has previously been in the minority, seems likely to become the majority, and when democratic parliamentarism threatens to turn on the very group, whose political dominance it hitherto secured?

If the arrangement according to vocations is meant as an organization on the basis of shared interests, then it has no prospect of becoming the primary and decisive factor in government as long as interests other than those particular to vocation predominate in reality. Whether justified or not, the property-less employees in the various—in fact, all—vocations feel a deeper commonality of interest with one another than with the capitalist employers of the same vocational group. Faced with this indisputable fact, employers are also compelled to form a community of interest that reaches across vocational boundaries. As long as these conditions persist, any corporative form of organization growing out of social relations themselves will hardly be capable of displacing the current parliamentary-democratic regime type without simultaneously moving toward an autocratic regime type, that is, in truth, towards the dictatorial rule of one class over another.

NOTE

1. See my *Problem des Parlamentarismus*, p. 21, and the literature cited there.

SIX

The Majority Principle

It is precisely the prevention of class domination for which the principle of the majority is suited. Already indicative is the fact that experience has shown the principle to be compatible with the protection of the minority. The very concept of a majority already presupposes the existence of a minority and, thus, the right of the minority to exist. Though this does not entail the necessity, it at least raises the possibility of a protection of the minority.

The protection of the minority is the essential function of so-called freedoms and fundamental rights or human and civil rights, which are guaranteed by all modern parliamentary-democratic constitutions. Originally, they were meant to protect the individual from the executive power,[1] which, still rooted in the legal principles of absolute monarchy, was authorized to infringe upon the sphere of the individual in the name of the "public interest," unless expressly forbidden by law. As soon as—as is the case in the constitutional monarchy and the democratic republic—both administration and adjudication are only possible on the basis of specific legal authorization, however, and the legality of execution emerges more and more clearly as a conscious principle, the establishment of freedoms and fundamental rights only makes sense on the precondition that it take on a specific constitutional form.[2] No conventional law, but only one produced in a qualified process can provide the basis for an infringement by the executive power upon the sphere that freedoms and fundamental rights build up around the individual. The typical way of qualifying constitutional laws vis-à-vis conventional laws is the requirement of a higher quorum and of a special—possibly two-thirds or three-quarters—majority.

Even though in theory such a distinction between conventional and constitutional law would be possible in a direct democracy as well, in practice only really the parliamentary legislative process comes into question for such a differentiation. In a popular assembly, the awareness of physical power is simply too great to allow for anything more than submission to an absolute majority. In the long run, an absolute majority here would not be willing to forgo the implementation of its will in the face of a qualified minority. Such a rational form of self-restraint can only be constitutionally instituted within the parliamentary process. Here, the purpose of the catalog of fundamental rights and freedoms changes from the protection of the individual from the state to the protection of a (qualified) minority from a merely absolute majority. Measures, which infringe upon certain national, religious, economic, or broadly intellectual spheres of interest, are possible only with the assent, and not against the will, of a qualified minority; that is, they require agreement between the majority and the minority. If it originally seemed as if the principle of the absolute majority accorded most closely with the realization of the idea of democracy, then it becomes apparent now that the principle of the qualified majority may under certain circumstances lead to an even closer approximation of the idea of freedom by introducing a certain tendency towards unanimity into the governmental process.

Here, the parliamentary process teaches us that, even with regard to the majority principle, we have to differentiate between ideology and reality. Ideologically—that is, in the system of the democratic ideology of freedom—the majority principle stands for government on the basis of the greatest possible agreement between the will of society and the wills of individual subjects. When the will of society agrees with more individual wills than it contradicts—and, as we have previously shown, this is the case with decisions made by majority rule—then the potential for freedom—in the sense of self-determination—has been maximized.

If one disregards the fiction that the majority somehow represents the minority and that the will of the majority is the will of all, then the majority principle comes to be perceived as a principle of domination by the majority over the minority. Yet, in reality, this is usually not the case. First of all, social reality militates against what is sometimes fittingly called "arithmetical coincidence." In actuality, it is not the numerical majority that is important. Even where the so-called majority principle is fully accepted, the numerical minority may well rule over the numerical majority. This fact, which may be concealed through some sort of electoral ingenuity that makes the ruling group falsely appear to be the majority or may, as in the case of a so-called minority government, not be concealed at all, contradicts the ideology of the majority principle and of democracy, but is nonetheless completely compatible with the latter's real form.

From the point of view of social reality, the majority principle does not mean that the will of the numerical majority prevails. Rather, its significance consists in the fact that, under the influence of this ideology, the individuals making up the social community are essentially divided into two groups. What is important here is that the tendency to form or to win a majority has the effect of overcoming the countless impulses in society, which push towards differentiation and division, and reduces them to a single, basic contradiction. This means that, in the end, essentially only two large groups struggling for power are left standing across from one another. Though the two groups may be more or less different with regard to their numerical strength, they do not differ all that much in their political significance and social potency. Initially, it is this force of social integration that sociologically characterizes the principle of the majority.

That the efficacy of the majority principle is not really dependent upon the idea of a numerical majority is most intimately related to the fact that absolute domination by the majority over the minority does not actually exist in social reality. The reason for this is that the will of society, which is produced according to the so-called majority principle, does not represent a dictate from the majority against the minority, but is rather the result of the mutual interaction between the two groups and a consequence of their colliding political persuasions. A dictatorship of the majority over the minority is already not possible, because a minority condemned to irrelevance will eventually abandon its—now merely formal and therefore not only worthless, but downright detrimental—participation in government. This would deprive the majority—which already by definition is impossible without a minority—of its very character.

That possibility is precisely what provides the minority with the means for gaining influence upon the decisions of the majority. This is especially true within a parliamentary democracy. After all, the entire parliamentary process, whose dialectical procedures are based on speech and counterspeech, argument and counterargument, aims for the achievement of compromise. Herein lies the actu-

al significance of the majority principle within a real democracy
and, hence, the former is more aptly described as a majority-*minority* principle. By dividing the entire body of subjects into essentially
two large groups, this principle has already furnished the possibility for compromise in government, since the final integration into a
majority, as well as a minority, itself necessitates compromise. Compromise means favoring that which binds over that which divides
those who are to be brought together. Every exchange and every
contract represents a compromise, because to compromise means to
get along [*vertragen*].

Even just a fleeting glance at parliamentary practice shows that,
particularly within the parliamentary system, the majority principle
proves valuable as a principle of compromise and of the balancing
of political differences. After all, the aim of the entire parliamentary
process is to achieve a compromise between opposing interests, to
produce a resultant of the various conflicting social forces. This process guarantees that the various interests of the groups represented
in parliament are given a voice, that they are able to manifest themselves as such in a public proceeding. If the specifically dialectical
process within parliament has a deeper meaning, then surely it is
that the opposition of the thesis and antithesis of political interests
somehow results in a synthesis. Here, however, this can only refer
to a compromise, and not—as those who confuse parliamentarism's
reality with its ideology allege—a "higher" absolute truth or an
absolute value standing above group interests.

It is from this standpoint that one must judge the question as to
what electoral system should be the basis for electing parliament,
i.e., which electoral scheme should be preferred from the standpoint
of parliamentary democracy: the majority system or the proportional representation system. The decision must be made in favor of the
latter, as an analysis of that system's political significance demonstrates: By demanding that the simultaneous filling of multiple [par-
liamentary] seats[3] should occur in such a way that each party has a
number of elected representatives corresponding to its strength, i.e.,
that every party is given its "own" proportional representation, one
abandons the notion that the "People" as a unitary whole creates
the representative body. The demand for an electoral system, whose
procedures ensure that each party is recognized in proportion to its
own strength, expresses the desire that not the entire electorate, but
only partial electoral bodies constitute the voting Subject. In
contrast to what happens in district-based electoral systems, these
electoral bodies are composed not according to an unnatural princi-

ple of territoriality, but according to the principle of personal status.[4] Not the inhabitants of an arbitrarily marked off area, but party members, i.e., people who share the same political persuasion, should constitute the bodies among which the available seats are distributed and through whose acts of will those seats are filled.[5]

Due to their composition, these electoral bodies are free from internal battles. Though the votes of a party do not have to be distributed evenly among its candidates (and here different types of proportional voting systems allow for different possibilities), the fact that the number of votes received by individual candidates within the same party can vary has a different meaning here than it does in an election held within the same electoral body but based instead on the majority principle. Just as the total number of votes cast by the members of one party in a proportional representation system are not in competition with, but parallel to the votes cast by those of another party, the votes cast for individual candidates within a party do not stand in a polarized, but rather in a parallel relationship to one another—they reinforce one another with regard to the final result. In the ideal case, there are no losers in a proportional vote, because no majorities are formed. To be elected, it is not necessary to receive a majority of the votes, but only a "minimum threshold," the calculation of which constitutes a specific technical feature of proportional representation.

If one looks at the full electoral result and compares the proportionally elected representative body in its entirety with the electorate as a whole, then in a certain sense one could say that this representation has come about with the votes of all and against the votes of none. In other words, it has come about unanimously—a fact that is occasionally cited as synonymous with the very nature of proportionality. Of course, this only applies to the ideal case. As a general rule, there will in fact be minorities who fail to obtain the minimum number of votes necessary to win a seat and, thus, go unrepresented.

The higher the number of open seats in relation to the number of votes cast, the more the idea of proportionality is realized. One possible extreme case is if there is only one open seat. It would be foolish to assume that the idea of proportionality could not be realized at all in such a case. For it would be satisfied if all voters cast their votes unanimously for one person—that is, if there is unanimity in its actual sense. The other extreme case, however, is if even the smallest imaginable party—consisting of only one voter—is proportionally represented. This would mean the end of the representative system as such, however, since there would have to be as many elected representatives as there are voters—i.e., the condition of direct democracy. The purpose of looking at these extreme cases is not to push the idea of proportional elections to absurdity, but rather to reveal the ultimate goals inherent in it and, therefore, to expose the fundamental principle, which makes proportional representation appear "just" to many people.

The aforementioned fundamental principle is that of freedom, i.e., of radical democracy. Just as I only want to obey a law that I have helped create, so I only want to recognize someone—if anyone at all—as my representative in government, if he was chosen for this position by, and not against, my will. Thus, the idea of proportionality becomes a part of democratic ideology, but its actual effects become a part of democracy's real form, parliamentarism.

This leads to the following consideration: If a pure majority system, unadulterated by the contingency of electoral districting, were used to elect parliament, then only the majority and no minority would be represented. Proportional representation basically represents nothing more than a rationalization of the very goal pursued by combining the majority system with the division into districts: an assurance of the existence of an opposition, without which the parliamentary process would be unable to fulfill its true purpose. Once this fact has been accurately recognized, however, it is no longer just a question of merely ensuring the existence of a minority in parliament. Rather, it becomes imperative that all political groups are represented in parliament in proportion to their respective strengths, so that the true constellation of interests is reflected by this body in the first place. This, after all, constitutes the principal precondition for the achievement of a compromise.

This line of thought also dispenses with the objection, often raised against the idea of proportionality, that it does not make sense to have minorities proportionally represented, if the decisions of parliament must ultimately rely on the principle of the majority anyway. The stronger the representation of the minority or minorities in parliament, the greater must be the influence that they by their very presence exert upon the formulation of the majority's will. Therefore, there can be no doubt that proportional representation actually amplifies that very tendency of freedom to prevent the will of majority from completely dominating the will of the minority.

An objection, which has been raised in particular against proportional representation, is that it encourages the formation of small, indeed the very smallest, parties and, thus, creates the danger of party fragmentation. This is correct and undoubtedly raises the possibility of no party having an absolute majority in parliament. Therefore, the achievement of a majority, which is an indispensable part of the parliamentary process, is made considerably more difficult. But viewed more closely, the effect of proportional representation in this regard is merely to transfer the necessity of party coalitions—that is, the necessity of laying aside smaller differences between the parties and instead agreeing on the most important common interests—from the electorate to the parliament. The political integration, which is inherent in party coalitions and compelled by the majority principle, is unavoidable and represents from a social-technical standpoint by no means an evil, but, on the contrary, a step forward. That this integration occurs more easily in parliament itself than within the broad mass of voters cannot be seriously denied. After all, the extensive differentiation into political interest groups facilitated by proportional representation must be seen as a necessary precondition for the [subsequent] effective integration guaranteed by the majority principle.

More than any other electoral system, proportional representation presupposes the organization of those who possess political rights into political parties. Where this organization has not yet sufficiently occurred, proportional representation has the explicit tendency to speed up and strengthen this process. Proportionality is a decisive step in a direction already alluded to before: that of making political parties constitutionally anchored organs of government. Even where it has not achieved this, however, it has an effect, which we have already recognized to be the consequence of dynamics that are fundamental to the democratic multiparty state. Here, government is not dominated by the interests of a single group, but is rooted rather in a process where many group interests organized into parties compete with one another as such and reach an equilibrium. But if government is not to be the expression of one-sided party interests, then preferably all parties must be guaranteed the ability to voice their interests and to compete with one another in order to reach a compromise eventually. A parliament based on proportional representation provides precisely this kind of guarantee.[6]

If one has recognized the real character of the majority principle that dominates the parliamentary process, then one is also able to judge correctly one of parliamentarism's most difficult and dangerous problems, the filibuster. Parliamentary rules and particularly the rights granted to the minority may be abused by that minority in order to hinder or even prevent the majority from passing undesirable resolutions by temporarily paralyzing the machinery of parliament. Insofar as this is achieved by making use of legitimate rules of procedure, such as long speeches, the provocation of roll call votes, or the filing for emergency motions that must take precedence over routine items on the daily agenda, one speaks of a "procedural" filibuster. Meanwhile, paralyzing the parliamentary process via the direct or indirect use of force, such as noisemaking, the destruction of fixtures, etc., is referred to as a "physical" filibuster. The latter already lacks any justification because of its formal illegality. But even the former must, insofar as it prevents any parliamentary decision-making at all, be viewed as running counter to the purpose and spirit of parliamentary procedures. To reject the filibuster entirely as incompatible with the majority principle, however, would require the latter's erroneous identification with majority domination. In fact, rather than preventing parliamentary decisions altogether, the filibuster has not infrequently served as a means for pushing the parliamentary process towards a compromise between the majority and the minority.

Here, a distinct difference between the real forms of democracy and autocracy becomes apparent. In the latter, there is no or at least a very limited possibility of balancing opposing political interests in government, since the opportunity for political currents and countercurrents is altogether lacking. It is in this way that democracy and autocracy differ from one another in their distinctive political-psychological situations. The mechanics of democratic institutions are directly aimed at raising the political emotions of the masses to the level of social consciousness, in order to allow them to dissipate. Conversely, the social equilibrium in an autocracy rests on the repression of these political emotions into a sphere, which may be compared to the subconscious on the individual psychological level. This easily leads—if one wants to make use of the modern psychoanalytic theory of repression—to a heightened disposition towards revolution.

That is why the subjection of the individual also has a slightly different meaning in an autocracy than it does in a democracy, or better put: it is generally accompanied by a different sentiment. The awareness that a law, to which I must submit myself, was made in part by a person whom I have elected, i.e., that it has come about with his or her agreement or at least with his or her participation in determining its content, may create a certain willingness to obey.

While this willingness is not necessarily absent in an autocracy, it nonetheless derives from a different psychological source. The democratic theory of a *contrat social*, the doctrine of a social contract, is certainly an ideological fiction. But in a real psychological sense, the social equilibrium in a democracy may in fact rest more on a degree of mutual agreement than it does in an autocracy where the only goal is to bear the shared burden of domination.

The use of the majority principle faces certain, almost natural, restrictions. The majority and the minority need to be able to understand one another if they are to come to an agreement. The factual preconditions for mutual understanding among those who participate in government must be present: This means a society that is relatively culturally homogenous and, in particular, shares the same language. If "nation" primarily refers to a cultural and linguistic community, then the majority principle only fully makes sense within a nationally homogenous body. From this it follows that in supra- and international communities, and especially in nationally heterogeneous states (so-called *Nationalitätenstaaten*), decisions regarding national-cultural questions cannot be left to the central parliament. Instead, they must be left to the autonomy—that is, the representative bodies—of the [various] national communities (subgroups), which are organized according to the principle of personal status. The familiar argument that the uniform application of the majority principle to the human community of today would necessarily lead to absurd results does not really strike at the principle as such, but merely at the excessive burden placed upon that principle by extensive centralization.

This is the same standpoint from which one must judge the Marxist view, which contends that the majority principle is only applicable to a society based upon a complete commonality of interest among its members, but not to one divided by class contradictions. The reason, it is argued, is that the majority principle may be suitable for resolving disagreements of a secondary—that is to say, merely technical—nature, but is incapable of resolving vital conflicts of interest.[7]

Let us set aside the fact that there exists no human society in which all interests automatically stand in a harmonious relationship to one another, but rather that such a relationship must be reinforced by constant and ever renewed compromises, since even the smallest disagreements can turn into vital conflicts of interest. The Marxist rejection of the majority principle as a basic feature of democracy and especially parliamentarism does not really rest upon any experiential insight into the principle's inadequacy for a class-divided society. Rather, it rests upon the—not rationally justifiable—desire to overcome class contradictions not through peaceful resolution, but rather through revolutionary violence—that is, not in a democratic, but rather in an autocratic-dictatorial manner. The majority principle is rejected, because—rightly or wrongly—compromise, for which the majority principle furnishes the precondition, is rejected. [Yet] in practice, compromise constitutes a real approximation to the unanimity that the idea of freedom demands in the development of the social order by its subjects, and, hence, the majority principle, in accordance with the idea of political freedom, proves valuable in this regard as well.

The theory of historical materialism teaches that social development will inevitably result in a situation where essentially only two groups are left standing across from one another, each a class with interests inimical to the other's. Further, a Marxist theoretician has recently demonstrated[8] that the relations between these two classes can reach—and, indeed, it appears must reach and already repeatedly have reached—a certain state of equilibrium, whose disruption or abrogation is unlikely for the foreseeable future. If these claims are indeed accurate, then the choice facing socialist theory is no longer, as it was often thought to be, one between formal democracy and dictatorship. For then, democracy is the only natural and adequate expression of the existing power relations and the one political form to which a society thusly constituted will repeatedly turn, even amid occasional, maybe even successful, attempts at dictatorship. For then, democracy is the point of rest to which the political pendulum, after swinging left and right, must return time and again.

If, as the Marxist critique of so-called bourgeois democracy avers, what really matters are the actual power relations in society, then the parliamentary-democratic state with its essentially bifurcative majority-minority principle is [in fact] the "true" expression of today's society with its division into essentially two classes. That such a powerful conflict exists may be regretted, but it cannot be denied. If there is a political form that provides the possibility of resolving this conflict peacefully and gradually, instead of pushing it to the point of catastrophe by violent revolutionary means, then surely it is the parliamentary-democratic form. The latter's ideology may be a socially unachievable freedom, but its reality is peace.

NOTES

1. [Here, I am using "executive power" to translate *vollziehende Gewalt.* The simpler *Vollziehung*, meanwhile, will usually be translated as "executive sphere."]

2. See my *Allgemeine Staatslehre*, p. 154ff.

3. [Here, as well as throughout the rest of the chapter, *Mandat* is translated as "seat."]

4. [*Personalitätsprinzip* is translated as "personal status." See Kelsen (Anders Wedberg, trans.), *General Theory of Law and State* (Union, NJ: Lawbook Exchange, Ltd., 1999), 305.]

5. From this it follows that the combination of proportional representation with the division into electoral districts (the territorial organization of the electorate) results in an internal contradiction. That which acts as a corrective within the majority system is in fact organically disruptive to proportional representation.

6. It should be mentioned, however, that proportional representation does pose a certain danger. Once political parties have achieved a certain permanence among those possessing political rights, so that significant shifts in the power relations among political groups are no longer to be expected in the foreseeable future; and once a two-party system—which in turn is favored by the parliamentarian principle of the majority—has directly or indirectly been formed; then proportional representation threatens to lead to a certain rigidity of the political system. The political group possessing a, even if only slim, majority permanently stays in power, while the other group is permanently condemned to the role of an opposition despite its significant influence. There is want of the possibility of a salutary change in governance [*Wechsel in der Regierung*], of a kind of back-and-forth system, in which the two dominant groups alternate in running, and, hence, in carrying the responsibility for, the state. An opposition that shortly before was itself in power and can hope to be so again soon has a very different, more understanding and benevolent, relationship with the governing majority, than an opposition that sees itself permanently shut out of running the state. In the latter instance, there arises the danger of a certain embitterment and, therefore, of a paralysis of the majority through the minority, which may not be strong enough to jump into the saddle itself, but nonetheless have enough strength to interfere with the majority's grip on the reins [of power].

In such a situation, dissatisfaction with proportional representation and a desire to go back to a majority system with electoral districts is somewhat understandable. Precisely because of the irrationality of the moment of contingency associated with it, the majority system provides the possibility that even a party that only commands a strong popular minority, may come to power under the aforementioned [two-]party constellation. For such a party may still be able to become a majority in parliament due to the arbitrariness of electoral districting, only [of course] to once again be relegated to the status of a minority and the role of an opposition by the same arbitrariness. For even if the strength of each party remains relatively constant within the state as a whole, shifts within individual districts are possible for a wide variety of reasons.

7. See Max Adler, *Die Staatsauffassung des Marxismus* (1923), p. 116ff., and my work *Sozialismus und Staat*, p. 123ff.

8. Otto Bauer, *Die österreichische Revolution* (1923), p. 16. See also my discussion of this work in *Kampf* (1924), p. 50, and Otto Bauer's response entitled "Das Gleichgewicht der Klassenkräfte," p. 57ff. See, furthermore, Max Adler, *Politische oder soziale Demokratie* (1920), p. 112ff.

SEVEN

Administration

The will of society or the social order does not operate on a single level, but essentially unfolds in (at least two) stages: the general norm and the individual act. The fact that one must differentiate between two completely different functions in the process of government creates—in conjunction with the law of the division of labor—a tendency for establishing a parliament-like organ in every state or state-like society; hence, it places limits on the ideological postulated [principle of] freedom.

The fact that the creation of the will of society occurs in stages results in a much more severe, and often overlooked, inhibition of freedom. One only became aware of this fact when the democratic parties, upon attaining power, attempted to bring about the social-technical realization of their ideal, i.e., of democracy. With the demand for freedom, one had hitherto contented oneself with a particular organization of the legislative organ (i.e., the organ responsible for the creation of general norms): [this entailed] universal, equal suffrage and referenda. Now, however, when this demand has been met, there has arisen the task of democratizing the second stage of the governmental process. Specifically, one has begun to postulate that the individual governmental functions of adjudication and administration, which are commonly subsumed under the term "execution" [*Vollziehung*], should also be democratically organized.

It is quite telling that the latter demand usually is made not by the majority parties that came to power on the basis of a democratic program, but rather by minority parties, which otherwise do not particularly emphasize the principle of democracy. Also telling is the fact that one and the same party may demand the democratization of the executive functions where it is a minority, but reject or only hesitatingly and with strong reservations acquiesce in this demand where the party commands a majority. The second attitude does not necessarily mean, however, that a democratic party does not stay true to the principle of democracy once it has attained power. On the contrary, it may actually be defending that principle. The unique structure of the governmental process with its division into stages and the dissimilar nature of these two successive [*sukzedierenden*] functions mean that the democratization of one stage produces an entirely different effect than does the democratization of the other. The one—the making of general norms, the so-called legislative sphere—is (relatively) unconstrained, while the other—the so-called executive sphere—is (relatively) constrained.[1] The executive sphere is essentially subject to the idea of legality, and this idea comes into conflict with democracy at a certain stage of government.

At first glance, it may appear that the democratic organization of the executive sphere simply follows from the democratic organization of the legislative sphere, and that the idea of democracy is served all the better, the further the democratic form of government seizes upon the process of execution. Yet, this is by no means the case. Even if legislative democracy is presupposed, this in no way proves that the legality of execution is best achieved through democratic means. Admittedly, the democratic election of the highest executive organs by parliament and their accountability to parliament provide a certain, though by no means the only possible, guarantee for the legal operation of these organs, i.e., for the fact that the will of the People is carried out. Yet, even as far as parliamentary accountability is concerned, it is evident that a more autocratic ministerial system, (i.e., execution through unitary organs) is more suitable in this regard. A collegial system of a specifically democratic nature not only would reduce the sense of accountability on the part of the individual, but also would render the enforcement of responsibility more difficult.

The incompatibility of the principle of legality with the principle of democracy grows more intense to the same extent that the organization of a larger society is accompanied by the socially irrefutable desire for decentralization, for a federal [*räumlich*] arrangement of the social body. In this regard too, the functional difference of the two stages, within which the governmental process operates, is evidenced. The issuance of specific acts of state, which is the province of the so-called executive sphere, is capable and in need of a much higher degree of decentralization than the act of general legislation [*genereller Willensbildung*], [which falls within] the so-called legislative sphere. And a radical democratization of the middle and lower levels, which are created by decentralization, actually threatens to lead to the abolition of the democratic organization of the legislative sphere.

[With decentralization] the state territory is divided into larger administrative regions (provinces), which in turn are divided into smaller administrative areas (districts). If, in accordance with the idea of democracy, the administration of these regions is assigned to collegial bodies elected by the regions' citizens, so that directly underneath the central executive [*Regierung*] there are provincial assemblies, under which, in turn, there are district assemblies, then it is more than likely that these self-governing administrative bodies do not view the legality of their acts as their highest goal. Rather, they will consciously seek to contradict the laws passed by the central parliament, particularly if their political make-up, that is, their internal power relations, is different from that of the central legislative body. The will of the whole expressed by the central legislature is in danger of being paralyzed by the wills of the parts expressed within the various self-governing administrative bodies. Even in its unnatural state where it signifies self-determination through majority rule, the idea of freedom maintains some of its originally anarchic tendency to dissolve the social whole into its individual atoms.

There certainly are organizational means for meeting this danger and overturning illegal acts of the democratically organized, self-governing administrative bodies. Yet, none of these means promote the democratic governance of the administrative regions; instead, they represent its restriction. Without a doubt, the legality of execution—and, given a democratic legislative sphere, the will of the People and, consequently, democracy itself—at the middle and lower levels is best assured not by self-governing administrative bodies, but rather by unitary organs appointed by and accountable to the center, i.e., by an autocratic organization of this particular aspect of government.

This also means, however, that, in consequence of the principle of legality, a bureaucratic system necessarily finds its way into the organizational structure of fundamentally democratic states. This is the deeper reason why even in states where democracy has become a politically indisputable principle, such as in the United States, [the level of] bureaucratization increases to the same degree that the administrative duties of the state, i.e., the functions of the executive sphere, grow larger in number. [Nonetheless] it would be a mistake to see in this nothing other than an attenuation of democracy. Only from a purely ideological and unrealistic standpoint do democracy and bureaucracy appear to be absolute opposites.[2] Under certain conditions, bureaucratization in fact represents the preservation of democracy. The precise reason for this is that the democratic principle in general can only capture the upper levels; it cannot, without calling itself (that is, its validity for the sphere of general legislation) into question, penetrate the lower levels of a process in which the body politic continually recreates itself.[3]

The functional contradiction, which exists between the democratic organization of the legislative sphere and that of the executive sphere, as well as the resulting tendency on the part of legislative democracy to ally itself with an autocratic-bureaucratic form of execution, is evidenced by the fact that a democratization of the executive and, in particular, the administrative spheres can only occur with a simultaneous loss of intensity with regard to the legal function's content. For if the danger of illegality is to be eliminated from the activities of democratically organized executive organs, viz. of the self-governing administrative bodies—noting that such bodies lack virtually all accountability and, thus, the most important guarantee of legality—then these activities must be limited to an area of discretionary action, which is not subject to regulation by the law. Only broad discretionary powers can ensure the beneficial operation of a democratically organized administrative sphere. This means, however, that administrative democracy holds within itself a strong tendency towards decentralization. The will of the parts can be given leeway only at the expense of the will of the whole.

When the task of enforcing the boundaries, which are placed upon the discretion of middle and lower organs, is transferred to autocratic organs (appointed by, or at least accountable to and removable by, the higher organs), then this signifies an acceptance of a mixed system of democratic and autocratic elements for the organization of the middle and lower administrative levels. Herein lies, after all, the peculiarity of constitutional monarchy—only that, there, the combination of the democratic with the autocratic form occurs on the highest level of government, i.e., the legislative sphere, and, hence, a paralysis of democracy through autocracy (and vice versa) is not out of the question. Where the principle of mixed government is limited to the middle and lower levels of a, at the highest level, purely democratic government, however, not an endangerment, but rather a strengthening of democracy is to be expected.

The idea of legality, though it places constraints on democracy, must nonetheless be upheld if democracy is to be realized. With this recognition must come the demand for all those institutional controls that guarantee the legality of execution and which only shortsighted demagoguery would reject as incompatible with democracy. Foremost among these is the subjection of administrative activities to judicial jurisdiction, which must be expanded and strengthened to the same degree that administrative acts fall to democratized (and therefore partisan) entities.

However, not only individual administrative acts but also general regulative norms and especially laws can and must be submitted to judicial control—the former with respect to their legality and the latter with respect to their constitutionality. This control falls under the jurisdiction of a constitutional court, whose function is all the more important for democracy, the more the enforcement of the constitution in the legislative process is in the eminent interest of the minority and the more the rules regarding quorum, a qualified majority, etc., serve—as we have already seen—to protect that minority. Hence, if the minority's political existence, which is so important for the very nature of democracy, is to be secure, that minority must have an opportunity to appeal, directly or indirectly, to the constitutional court. Otherwise, the minority would be subject to the arbitrary will of the majority and the constitution would be a *lex imperfecta*. The fate of modern democracy depends to a large extent on a systematic development of all types of institutional controls. Democracy without [such] controls is impossible in the long run; the abandonment of that very self-restraint, which the principle of legality represents, means the breakdown of democracy itself.[4]

If the democratic principle—in the interest of its own self-preservation—must essentially be limited to the legislative process and to the selection of the highest executive organs, that is, if it must not penetrate that part of government commonly referred to as the executive sphere (judicial jurisdiction and administration), then this simultaneously demarcates the sphere beyond which the influence of political parties must not reach. The principle of legality, to which all aspects of the executive sphere must necessarily be subject, precludes any partisan influence on the executive functions of the courts, as well as of the administrative authorities.

Chapter 7

This is the only legitimate meaning that the demand for a "de-politicization" of state functions within a democracy—indeed, within any state—can have. Only qualified in this way does such a demand make sense. A de-politicization of the legislative sphere would mean its abolition, since the determination of the content of law can only occur in one of two ways: through the dictatorship of only one group interest or through a compromise among several group interests. For the simple fact that the act of legislation elevates a particular political value to the level of positive law and adopts a particular—even if one-sided—political direction in accordance with constitutional requirements, the execution of law can no longer be subject to the struggle between opposing political interests. Hence, the legitimate demand for de-politicization, in the limited sense of the elimination of partisan influences from the executive sphere, is entirely compatible with the broadest possible recognition of political parties and their integration into the constitution. Indeed, it is precisely in this way that one can place limits upon the unlawful activities of political parties. Their sphere of influence is the legislative [sphere] [*Legislative*], not the executive [sphere] [*Executive*].

Just like democracy, autocracy tends in practice to develop a collegial—and, hence, parliamentary—organ, which is based on the division of labor, for its legislative activities. On the other hand—and again like democracy and in part for the same reasons—it inevitably creates a bureaucracy for its executive functions. Hence, the actual structures of modern states tend to converge to some degree, as soon as these states have surpassed a certain minimum size and a certain level of civilization. This convergence in actual conditions occurs despite the persistence of contradictory ideologies. Just as with constitutional matters (that is, with regard to the method or form of government), the same tendency towards uniformity can also be ascertained in the content of norms, that is, in the area of substantive law. These days, the fact that the civil and criminal legal codes of modern states have grown ever more similar can hardly be denied.

NOTES

1. [In general (unless where noted otherwise), *Gesetzgebung* and *Vollziehung* will be consistently translated as "legislative sphere" and "executive sphere," respectively, as this seems to fit best with Kelsen's spatial division of government (i.e., the creation of the will of society or of the state) into "stages."]

2. Compare the divergent view taken by me on this point as recently as my first edition of this work, p. 23ff.

3. See Adolf Merkl, *Democratie und Verwaltung* (1923) and my *Allgemeine Staatslehre*, p. 361ff.

4. See, in this regard, my work *La garantie jurisdictionnelle de la constitution* ([originally in] *Revue du Droit public et de la science politique en France et à l'Etranger*, 1928) (Paris: Marcel Giard, 1928), p. 54ff.

EIGHT
The Selection of Leaders

Having familiarized oneself with the factual conditions that typically exist within so-called democratic states and having confronted these conditions with the democratic ideology of freedom, one may initially come to wonder how such an extraordinary tension between ideology and reality is at all possible in the long run. One may be led to believe that it is the peculiar function of democratic ideology to maintain the illusion of a freedom that is untenable in social reality—as if a high-pitched song of freedom emanating from the eternal depths of the human soul were trying to drown out the dull musical motif of social reality's brass chains.

The democratic ideology of freedom appears to play a similar role vis-à-vis its corresponding social reality as the ethical illusion of a free will does vis-à-vis the psychological insight that all human willing is inescapably subject to causal constraints. Between these two problem complexes there exists not just a superficial parallel, but a deeply intimate relationship. If one attempted to understand the social reality referred to as democracy only in terms of its own ideology, then Rousseau would actually be correct in his pessimism. But one cannot confine oneself to ascertaining the internal logic and meaning of the ideology, and then simply take them to be synonymous with the logic and meaning of the reality, upon which that ideology is contingent. Instead, one must seek to discover the reality's own significance and regulative principles, which, though not entirely independent from the ideology, may still be very different from it. In other words, one must seek to understand not only the subjective, but also the objective meaning of social events.

The idea of democracy corresponds to the absence of leadership, the spirit of which is reflected in the words, with which Plato has Socrates answer the question of how a man of exceptional quality, a genius, should be treated in the ideal state: "[W]e should bow down before him as someone holy, wonderful, and pleasing, but we should tell him that there is no one like him in our city and that it isn't lawful for there to be. We should pour myrrh on his head, crown him with wreaths, and send him away to another city" (*Republic,* III: 9).[1] Leadership has no place in an ideal democracy. Yet, the democratic freedom ideal, the absence of rule and, hence, of leadership, cannot be realized even approximately; social reality *is* rule and leadership.

The only question here can be how that rule is structured and how the leader is chosen. In this regard, democracy is characterized not by the fact that the ruling will is the will of the People, but rather that a broad segment of the subjects, that the largest possible number of the community's members, participates in government. Even this participation, however, is generally limited to a certain stage of the process (commonly referred to as the legislative sphere) and consists only in the creation of the legislative organ. This means that the specific function of the leaders, who rise above the mass, is limited to the execution of law. The executive [*Regierung*]—which is the political-legal form of leadership—is certainly capable of significantly influencing the legislative sphere. Already telling, however, is the fact that in order to do so, it must make use of another organ. The parliamentary mechanism, which is characterized by the conflict between majority and minority, presents an effective and real barrier even to an executive that enjoys majority support—a not inconsiderable difference from the political situation where the regent himself makes the laws that he, or rather the bureaucratic apparatus below him, then executes.

Admittedly, the creation of a collegial legislative organ is, as we have emphasized earlier, a universally observable tendency that arises out of the very nature of government. If the differentiation between such a parliamentary organ and the executive organ, as well as the resulting binding and constraining force on the executive, are seen as distinguishing features of real democracy, then the tendency toward democratic forms can be viewed as a developmental tendency common to all modern states. Simultaneously inherent in this tendency, however, is that particular institutional differentiation, which the theory of the separation of powers has already sought to articulate.

Considering the conflict between ideology and reality, the question of whether the separation of powers is a democratic principle cannot be answered definitively. From the standpoint of ideology, such a separation of powers, where the legislative and executive functions are divided among different organs, does not accord with the idea that the People should only be ruled by itself.[2] For, from that thesis it must follow that all powers and, thus, all governmental functions should be unified in the People or at least in a parliament representing the People. Furthermore, the political intention behind the dogma of the separation of powers since Montesquieu was never to pave the way for democracy. Quite the opposite: It was meant to provide the monarch, who had been nearly eliminated from the legislative sphere by democratic forces, with an opportunity in the executive sphere to continue to exercise power.

The dogma of the separation of powers is a crucial feature of the ideology of constitutional monarchy—hence the curious constitutional (that is, monarchist) theory of the parity, equality, and independence of the executive sphere vis-à-vis the legislative sphere, even though that theory is completely incompatible with the idea and nature of the executive power [*Vollziehung*] reserved to the monarch. This theory proves highly effective in the praxis of constitutional monarchy: Given the power dynamics within such a state, the separation of powers means that the many-membered legislative organ, in which the People is alone represented, is by no means capable of asserting itself as the highest organ. If the executive power is assigned to a monarch and made equal, not subordinate, to the legislature, then experience shows that this monarch will emerge as a force superior to the representative body that participates in the making of law.

What becomes apparent here is a political overestimation of the legislative function. It is almost a matter of historical irony when a republic such as the United States of America faithfully adopts the dogma of the separation of powers and carries it to its extreme in the very name of democracy. Admittedly, the position of president in the United States is a conscious imitation of the position of king in England. In a so-called presidential republic, the executive power is assigned to a president who is not appointed by the representative body, but rather is directly elected by the People. If the independence of the president from the representative body is ensured in all other ways as well, then the principle of popular sovereignty is—as paradoxical as it may seem—weakened, rather than—as was presumably intended—strengthened. Where there is only one elected individual for millions of voters, the idea of popular representation must lose every last pretense of legitimacy. In a many-membered parliament where all popular parties are represented, the interaction of all these forces may still be able to produce something like a will of the People. However, in the case of a president, who is directly elected by popular vote and, thus, completely independent from parliament, but who cannot be controlled by a populace too massive to take action, the emergence of a will of the People is as unlikely as it is in the case of a hereditary monarch. Indeed, the chances of an—even if temporary—autocracy are greater in the former case than they are in the latter case. The method of selection does not play a decisive role.

Just how little connection there is between the idea of representation and the principle of democracy can be discerned from the fact that autocracy makes use of the same fiction. Just like the monarch and especially the absolute monarch, so every official appointed by the monarch passes for an organ of the state and, thus, a representative of the entire populace. There has never been a usurper or tyrant, who has not sought to justify his rule in this way. The autocratic rule of an absolute monarch, who seeks to legitimate himself with the idea of representation, and the pseudo-democratic rule of an elected "emperor" do not differ all that greatly from one another.

Nonetheless, the separation of powers can also be seen to produce effects that tend in a democratic direction. First of all, it prevents the concentration of state power, which would otherwise encourage that power's expansion and arbitrary exercise. In addition, however, it strives to insulate the sphere of general legislation from the direct influence of the executive, while at the same time opening up that sphere to direct popular influence. In the meantime, the function of the executive is reduced to the enforcement of law.

This does not actually mean that rule is "minimized" however. Rather, one should assume—if one may use the metaphor—that the sum of the social energies, which manifest themselves in political rule, remains constant in the transition from the autocratic to the democratic form of state, and that this transition merely constitutes a kind of redistribution of the power to rule, which was previously concentrated in a single point. This redistribution makes that power seem less burdensome from a subjective standpoint. [But] just because the dominant will is produced by the interaction of a majority of organs does not mean that it will lose any of its intensity.

Of course, the idea of leadership becomes obscured by the fact that the executive must be thought of as subordinate to a parliament with several hundred members; the power to rule shifts from a single leader to a multitude of persons, among whom the function of leadership, that is, of the creation of the ruling will, is divided. This means that the creation of many leaders becomes the central problem for real democracy, which—in contrast to its ideology—is not a leaderless society. It is not the lack, but the abundance of leaders that in reality differentiates democracy from autocracy. Thus, a special method for the selection of leaders from the community of subjects becomes essential to the very nature of real democracy. This method is the election.

A sociological analysis of this special democratic function is crucial for understanding the nature of real democracy. And in the course of that analysis, we once again run into the same problem we already faced in our general analysis of democracy: the divergence between ideology and reality. From the standpoint of democratic ideology, the election is seen as the transference of the will of the voter to those for whom he votes. Interpreted in this way, however, the election, and, hence, the democracy based upon it, would be, as has been said, a "logical impossibility"; for, in reality, the will is not transferable—*celui qui délègue, abdique*. Rousseau himself already showed that one's will cannot be represented.

This ideological interpretation of the election clearly derives from the desire to maintain the fiction of freedom. Since a will must only be governed [*bestimmen*] by itself if it is to remain free, the ruling will created by those who are elected must be seen as identical to the will of the voters—hence the fictitious identification of voters with their representatives. However, an objective analysis of the election must not let itself be misled by subjective ideology. The realistic interpretation of this function is a different one.

From a purely formal standpoint, the election essentially turns out to be a method for the creation of organs that, in contrast to other methods, is characterized by two moments: First, it is not a simple, but an aggregate function in which a number of constituent organs interact with one another. Second, the organ created by the election stands above those organs which created it, since it is the former that then articulates the ruling will, i.e., the norms, to which voters must submit. With these two moments, the election stands in direct contrast to the official appointment [*Ernennung*], which is the method for the creation of organs specific to real autocracy.

Particularly the second of the two aforementioned characteristics of the election—the fact that the followers choose the leader, i.e., that those subject to norms create the authority from which those norms emanate—is one reason for the ideological fiction of will transference. As psychological, viz. psychoanalytic, research has shown, social authority is imagined as a patriarchal authority. Just like religious (or any other) authority, social authority is originally experienced in the same manner as the very first authority that enters into the life of the developing person: as a father, a founding father, or a Divine Father. The psychological roots of social authority thus militate against the notion that authority can be created by those who are subject to it. For this notion means to say that the father is created by his children, that the creator is produced by those whom he has created.

In the primitive practice of totemism, clan members periodically don masks depicting their holy totemic animal, the primal father of the clan, during certain orgiastic festivals, so that they themselves temporarily play the father and cast off all bonds of social order. Similarly, democratic ideology wraps the People, which is comprised of subjects, in the mantle of authority, which remains inalienable and whose functional transference to those who are elected must be continually renewed. Even the theory of popular sovereignty is nothing more than a—even if very refined and sublimated—totemic mask.[3]

Next to the formal characteristics that have already been sketched out, however, the true face [of the election] reveals the following traits: In a democratic "election," the leader is not only chosen by the subjects, but he is selected from their midst. What has been so fittingly described as autocephalous selection [*Autokephalie*] by Max Weber is highly characteristic of real democracy and differentiates this state of affairs from the political organization referred to as autocracy (or, as of late, dictatorship). The ideology of the latter paints the leader as standing above the social community, which he rules, as an entirely different, namely higher, being, who is surrounded by a halo of divine origin or of magical powers. According to autocratic ideology, the leader is an organ that is not and in fact cannot be created by society. Rather, he must be imagined as the force that first brings society into being, as an entity with humanly incomprehensible origins. In the system of autocratic ideology, the origin, selection, and creation of the leader are beyond question and cannot be objects for or captured by rational inquiry. Leadership here represents an absolute value, which is expressed in the deification of the leader.

Reality though confronts this ideology with an extremely embarrassing problem when the leader dies. In truly ideological fashion, this difficulty is sometimes covered up by bestowing the notion of the leader not upon the person of the mortal monarch, but rather — as, for example, in the Hungarian constitution — upon an abstraction such as the eternal holy crown. [In contrast,] the reality of the matter is marked by the usurpation of power, which is equivalent to a kind of self-creation on the part of the ruling organ. Where there exists a notion of succession, yet the previous dictator has failed to designate an heir and no succession takes place, the leader is not selected from the domestic population, but rather from abroad (heterocephalous selection [*Heterokephalie*]).

In the system of democratic ideology, the notion of leadership is the focus of rational reflection. It represents not an absolute, but only a relative value. The leader counts as a "leader" only for a certain length of time and in particular ways. Otherwise, he is no different from his fellows and is subject to criticism. This explains why here the actions of the leader are made public, while in an autocracy they are kept secret. The leader in an autocracy transcends society, while the leader in a democracy is immanent to society. Hence, the individual exercising the leadership function in an autocracy is characteristically seen as standing above and not below the social order and thus essentially lacks all accountability. Meanwhile, the accountability of leaders constitutes a specific feature of real democracy. Most importantly, however, leadership in a democracy cannot become the permanent monopoly of the individual or of the few, since leadership is not some kind of supernatural quality, but a position that is conferred. Real democracy thus factually evidences a more or less rapid turnover of leaders.

Certainly, a tendency on the part of the leader to assert the permanence of his position can be observed here as well. But here this tendency is met with a resistance, which is not least rooted in ideology and which becomes operative in people's psyches as a motivation for their behavior. The rationalization of leadership and its consequences — publicity, criticism, accountability, and the belief that the leader can be freely chosen — make the permanence of the leader impossible. To the degree that a leader does become permanent, however, the ideology of leadership also changes.

Real democracy is thus marked by a constant upward flow that moves from the community of subjects to the leadership positions.

(To avoid misunderstanding, it should be noted that this refers not so much to the leadership of parties, but rather to the leadership of the state manifested in the form of the state's executive [*Staatsregierung*].) This highly characteristic movement clearly differentiates real democracy from autocracy, where the possibility of upward mobility is nonexistent or at least very limited. Instead, one is trapped in a relatively static power relation. In comparison, the specifically democratic method for the selection of leaders represents a significant expansion of the pool upon which this process is able to draw; in other words, it expands the number of individuals competing for the leadership position.

Since both democracy and autocracy are only methods for the creation of a social order, proponents of each these principles believe that theirs is able to produce the best order. Hence it is a completely hollow and meaningless—if always highly popular— argument to say that democracy does not stand a chance against autocracy because the latter represents the only plausible principle that the best, and only the best, should rule. The "best": In the present context, this can only refer to those who produce the best norms; and the best norms are precisely the norms that alone should be produced. The catch phrase of "rule by the best" turns out to be a wretched tautology. It is not a question of whether the best should rule—on this point proponents of both autocracy and democracy agree. The actual problem is a political, namely social-technical, one: how the best (singular or plural) can come, or lay claim, to power. It is the method for the creation of the leaders that is crucial.

Precisely in this regard the proponents of the autocratic ideal have nothing to offer against democracy, however. After all, the autocratic system as just depicted does not, strictly speaking, have a method for creating leaders. Instead, it covers up the most important problem in politics with a mystical-religious veil, which conceals the birth of the divine hero from the profane masses. In truth, this means that the answer to the question of who should become leader and how they should do so is left to the arbitrariness of force. But even for democracy, a conscientious examination of its method for selecting leaders will not be able to offer up anything decisive.[4]

It is charged that democracy helps loud-mouths and demagogues, who play on the worst instincts of the masses, to attain power. To this one may give the pointed response that it is precisely the method of democracy that places the fight for leadership [positions] on the broadest possible foundation by making leadership an object of public competition in the first place. Hence, the democratic method first provides a basis—indeed, the greatest possible basis—for the selection of leaders. Meanwhile, the autocratic principle—particularly in its real form as a bureaucratic monarchy—does little to guarantee that the way will be clear for capable individuals [to rise to leadership]. Furthermore, democracy, which facilitates the rise to leadership, simultaneously guarantees that a leader who proves incompetent is quickly removed, while, in an autocracy, the principles of life tenure and the heritability of [political] functions have the exact opposite effect.

Very closely related in this regard is the fact that in a democracy, where the fundamental need to prove oneself and the freedom to criticize dominate, defects in public administration are easily and quickly revealed, while in an autocracy, where the conservation of the authority of its functionaries is the dominant principle, a traditional system of concealment develops. This is the reason why short-sighted observers see a greater degree of corruption in a democracy than in an autocracy. Surely, it is a great blessing when an intelligent and moral person is allowed to become an absolute monarch. Yet, just as history evidences politically and culturally blossoming democracies next to those befallen by internal decay, it also shows in its impartial equanimity, next to the ideal of glorious emperors, frightful images of debauched Caesars, who destroy their own states and cause their Peoples unspeakable misery.

In social reality, the idea of freedom, which is the primary principle of democracy, is transformed from a rejection of leadership into the idea that leadership should be open to everyone. Likewise, democracy's secondary principle of the fundamental equality of individuals is transformed into a tendency toward possible equalization. The demagogic assumption that all citizens are equally capable of performing any particular political function eventually becomes [a positing of] the mere possibility that all citizens can be made capable of performing these functions. In practice, civic education becomes one of democracy's principal demands.[5] All education, it is true, is based on the relationship between teacher and student—an intellectual form of the leader-follower relation—and therefore (in a good sense) essentially authoritarian in character. Nevertheless, the problem of democracy presents itself in social practice as an educational problem on the grandest scale.[6]

The question regarding the ability of a particular class to rule or to share in the rule of the state must also be judged from this standpoint. This question does, and indeed should, arise. One of the faults of the socialist theory of proletarian dictatorship is that it—understandably—imagines the social revolution as analogous to the bourgeois revolutions of 1789 and 1848 and, therefore, naturally assumes that the proletariat is just as capable of seizing power as the bourgeoisie was in its time.[7] The fact is, however, that the bourgeoisie was able—thanks to its economic situation—to prepare itself for the political power, from which the aristocracy had kept it away. It may be a matter of tragic fate that in those places where political power has thus far been seized by the proletariat, it has inevitably fallen into hands, which are unequal to the task and, thus, unable to hold on to that power permanently. Not only the administrative catastrophe in the Russian Socialist Republic is meant here, but also the extraordinary difficulties experienced by the Social Democratic Party, which is led by descendants of the bourgeoisie, in Germany as well as Austria. These difficulties are rooted in the fact that the proletariat cannot provide the party with the qualified personnel necessary for taking over the administrative apparatus even to that limited degree required by a bourgeois-socialist coalition government [*Regierungskoalition*].

NOTES

1. [The translation is taken from John M. Cooper, *Plato: Complete Works* (Indianapolis: Hackett Publishing Company, 1997), 1035 (398a).]

2. It was already pointed out by Hasbach (loc. cit., p. 17) that Montesquieu's theory of the separation of powers is incompatible with the idea of popular sovereignty.

3. See my essay "Gott und Staat" in *Logos: Internationale Zeitschrift für Philosophie der Kultur* (XI/3), p. 261ff.

4. It is not my intention in this text to argue that democracy guarantees the best process for choosing leaders, but merely to highlight the distinctiveness of the democratic vis-à-vis the autocratic method. In response to a value judgment which I had inappropriately offered on this point in favor of democracy, Reinhold Horneffer has correctly accused me of inconsistency in his work *Hans Kelsen's Lehre von der Demokratie* (Erfurt, 1926), p. 77f. If I decide in favor of democracy, it is solely for the reasons developed in the last chapter of the current work: the relation between the democratic form of state to a relativistic worldview. This is a position I had already taken in my *Allgemeine Staatslehre*, a fact that Horneffer appears to have overlooked.

5. See, in this regard, my essay "Politische Weltanschauung und Erziehung," in *Annalen für soziale Politik und Gesetzgebung* (2/1, 1912), p. 1ff.

6. See, in this regard, Steffen, loc. cit., p. 97.

7. Loc. cit., pp. 148, 149.

NINE

Formal versus Social Democracy

Marxists differentiate between a democracy based on the principle of the majority and a social, proletarian democracy. The former is understood as formal and bourgeois and the latter as a social order, in which subjects are given not only an equal share in government, but also in some sense an equal share in material goods. This differentiation must be categorically rejected. Freedom, not equality, primarily defines the idea of democracy.

The idea of equality certainly plays its own role in democratic ideology. Yet, as we have seen, it does so only in a completely negative, formal, and secondary sense. The demand for preferably universal, and therefore equal, freedom requires universal, and therefore equal, participation in government. Historically, the fight for democracy has been a fight for political freedom, that is, for popular participation in the legislative and executive spheres. Insofar as the idea of equality is meant to connote anything other than formal equality with regard to freedom (i.e., political participation), that idea has nothing to do with democracy. This can be seen most clearly in the fact that not the political and formal, but the material and economic equality of all can be realized just as well—if not better—in an autocratic-dictatorial form of state as it can in a democratic form of state. Completely apart from the fact that the equal share of goods, which "social" democracy is supposed to guarantee to all citizens, always refers to an ample share, the concept of equality can take on such diverse meanings that it is simply impossible to link it with the concept of democracy in any fundamental way.

This "equality" is meant to be synonymous with justice, and it proves to be just as ambiguous of a term. Marxist theory, or at least one of its newer variants, the Bolshevist doctrine, seeks to replace the ideology of freedom with the ideology of justice in the name of "democracy." But it is a clear misuse of terminology when the word "democracy," which both ideologically and practically represents a particular method for the creation of the social order, is used instead to describe that social order's content, which bears no essential connection to the method by which it was created. This kind of terminological manipulation has the ominous—even if unintentional—effect that the legitimating power and emotional value, which accompany the catchword of democracy thanks to its ideology of freedom, comes to benefit a state of outright dictatorship. In consequence of this social, as opposed to formal, conception of democracy, the difference between democracy and dictatorship is simply denied and dictatorship, which supposedly realizes social justice, is declared to be the "true" democracy. This has the side-effect of unjustly disparaging the democracy of today and, hence, the contribution of the group that—in part, very much against its own interests—brought about that democracy.

The fact that the democratic method is thrown overboard in the implementation of the socialist ideal in particular must seem strange. After all, socialism since Marx and Engels has proceeded from the assumption—fundamental not only to its political theory up to that point, but also to its economic theory—that the exploited and impoverished proletariat constitutes the majority of the population and that this proletariat must simply become conscious of its class character in order to organize itself within the socialist party for the class struggle against a vanishing minority. Only for this reason was socialism in particular able to demand democracy, for in a democracy, where the majority decides who rules, socialism's rise to power appeared inevitable.

Yet, the rise of bourgeois democracies in the first half of the nineteenth century and, even more so, their certain survival as well as their progressive democratic evolution in the following years were already no longer entirely compatible with socialist assumptions. Why does a merely political democracy not also develop into an economic democracy (that is, why does a bourgeois-capitalist group, not a proletarian-communist group, rule), when the socialist-minded proletariat constitutes the majority and universal, equal suffrage should secure it control of parliament?

Of course, this question is only valid where real democracy prevails and the universality and equality of political rights are unquestionably ensured. But in the great democracies of Western Europe and America, and basically in Germany and Austria as well, this is [in fact] the case. Citing electoral practices—such as the geometry of electoral districts, the practice of obstructing certain categories of voters from exercising their right to vote, and the like—and pointing to the powerful influence of the capitalist media are by no means sufficient to account for this situation. Bourgeois democracy remains stuck at the level of mere political equality, and that political equality does not lead to economic "equality." The reason for this—as the latest revolution, especially in Russia, visually demonstrates—is that the proletariat, which is interested in economic equality and the consequent nationalization or socialization of [the means of] production, does not (or not yet), contrary to the decades-old tenet of socialist theory, constitute the overwhelming majority of the People. Indeed, even where socialism has managed to seize absolute power through the proletariat, the latter only constitutes a weak minority.

Herein lies the reason for the fundamental change in the political methods of a part of the socialist party. It is the reason why democracy—which Marx and Engels viewed as not only compatible with the dictatorship of the proletariat, but indeed as the very form which that dictatorship would take—was necessarily replaced by a dictatorship embodying the absolute rule of a political dogma and of the party representing that dogma. Thus, the left wing of the proletarian party has abandoned the democratic ideal, since it believes that the proletariat will not, at least for the foreseeable future, be able to seize power under such a political form. Meanwhile, the right wing of the bourgeois parties also abandons the ideal, since it believes that this political form will no longer (or at least not much longer) allow the bourgeoisie to defend its [position of] power. All of this is clearly symptomatic of the fact that the strength of both groups is reaching an actual point of equilibrium.[1]

NOTE

1. See note 7, chapter 3.

TEN

Democracy and Philosophy

If, as the preceding discussion shows, democracy is only a form, a method for the creation of the social order, particularly then its value—insofar as this now becomes a matter of concern as well—appears extremely problematic. The specific procedure of creation, the particular form of a state or society, in no way addresses the apparently much more important question regarding the content of the state order. A solution to the social problem seems to depend on how the state or social order should be substantively organized—whether socialist or capitalist—and on whether that order should penetrate deeply into the sphere of the individual or, instead, be limited to a minimum. In short, the question is not so much how norms should be created, but rather what those norms should posit. Is it not a case of unduly emphasizing form over content, when the political discussion almost exclusively revolves around the choice between democracy and autocracy? But this is the way in which democracy in particular tends to formulate the problem, while autocracy—for reasons that have already been discussed—instead suppresses questions over forms of state.

Let us assume, however, that the state order should be exclusively governed by its subjects and that, thus, the question over the form of state has been decided. Only now are we confronted with the real question: What content should the People give to the laws, which it has itself created? Even radical democrats could not in good faith claim that resolving the question regarding the state's form also resolves the issue over the state's content, i.e., its correct and best content. Such an assertion could only be made by those holding the view that the People, and only the People, are in possession of the truth and have insight into what is good. Such a view can hardly have its origin in anything other than a religious-metaphysical hypothesis, which asserts that the People, and only the People, attains its wisdom in some supernatural way. This would amount to a belief in the divine right of the People—an idea as ridiculous and impossible as a belief in the divine right of kings.

In fact, various apologists for the idea of popular sovereignty have made similar claims. Even Rousseau is not far from doing so, when he justifies the binding nature of majority decisions, i.e., the authority of the majority, on the basis that the minority has erred regarding the true content of the *volonté générale*. But everyone suspects that the defenders of democracy are making use of an argument here, which is foreign to the very nature of democracy. That which was able to demand popular acceptance due to a single leader's charisma cannot be transferred to the many of the anonymous mass, to the average citizen: the claim of a highly personal relationship to the Absolute or to God, as whose messenger, instrument, or son the autocrat appears. Any serious attempt on the part of democracy to justify itself in this way would make it the donkey in lion's skin.

On the other hand, one does not have to become a pessimist and agree with Ibsen's bitter conclusion that the majority is always wrong and that, hence, popular insight into what is right is an utter impossibility. It is enough to doubt whether only the People, i.e., only the majority, is capable of knowing what is true and good, for one to take at least a skeptical stance toward democracy. In fact, the [very] assumption that knowledge of absolute truth and insight into absolute values are possible confronts democracy with a hopeless situation. For what else could there be in the face of the towering authority of the absolute Good, but the obedience of those for whom it is their salvation? There could only be unconditional and grateful obedience to the one who possesses—i.e., knows and wills—this absolute Good. This obedience, of course, can only rest on the belief that the authoritative figure of the lawmaker possesses the absolute Good insofar as the great multitude of subjects is denied that same knowledge.

It is precisely at this point, where all hope of legitimizing democracy appears to be lost, that its actual defense must begin. For this is the big question: Whether knowledge of absolute truth and insight into absolute values are actually possible. The conflict between democracy and autocracy becomes a conflict between worldviews, between life philosophies. The belief in absolute truth and absolute values furnishes the precondition for a metaphysical and, in particular, a religious-mystical worldview. The negation of this precondition, however, is the viewpoint that only relative truths and values are accessible to human cognition and that, consequently, every truth and every value must—just as the human individual who finds them—be prepared to abdicate its position and make room for others. This standpoint leads to a critical or positivist worldview, where the latter is understood as that philosophical and scientific school of thought, which takes the positive—i.e., that which is given and perceptible—and experience—changeable and constantly in flux—as its starting point. It thus rejects the assumption of an Absolute which transcends experience. This conflict of worldviews corresponds to a conflict between values and especially between basic political attitudes. The metaphysical-absolutistic worldview is linked to an autocratic, and the critical-relativistic to a democratic disposition.[1]

He who views absolute truth and absolute values as inaccessible to the human understanding cognition must deem not only his own, but also the opinion of others at least as feasible. The idea of democracy thus presupposes relativism as its worldview. Democracy values everyone's political will equally, just as it gives equal regard to each political belief and opinion, for which the political will, after all, is merely the expression. Hence, democracy offers every political conviction the opportunity to express itself and to compete openly for the affections of the populace. That is why the dialectical process in both the popular assembly and parliament, which is based on speech and counterspeech and paves the way for the creation of norms, has been identified—not incorrectly—as being democratic. The rule of the majority, which is so characteristic of democracy, distinguishes itself from all other forms of rule in that it not only by its very nature presupposes, but actually recognizes and protects—by way of basic rights and freedoms and the principle of proportionality—an opposition, i.e., the minority. The stronger the minority, however, the more the politics in a democracy become politics of compromise. Similarly, there is nothing more characteristic of the relativistic worldview than the tendency to seek a balance between two opposing standpoints, neither of which can by itself be adopted fully, without reservation, and in complete negation of the other.

The relativity of any value espoused by a particular political creed and the impossibility of a claim to absolute validity by a political program or ideal, even if backed by full subjective devotion and personal conviction, necessarily require the rejection of political absolutism as well—whether it be the absolutism of a monarch, a caste of priests, aristocrats, or warriors, a class, or any other privileged group.

He who in his political desires and actions is able to lay claim to divine inspiration or otherworldly enlightenment may well be right to be deaf to the voices of his fellows. He may be right to force his will as the will of the absolute Good upon a world of disbelievers and—because they want anything different—blind men. This is how the slogan of the divine-right theory of Christian monarchies, "authority, not the majority," came into being.

This slogan, however, has become a target for everything that aims for intellectual freedom, for a science that is free from mysticism and dogma and instead grounded in human reason and doubtful criticism, and—politically—for democracy. He who only relies on earthly truth and only allows human knowledge to direct social policy can justify the coercion, which the realization of that policy inevitably requires, in no other way than with the assent of at least the majority of those who are supposed to benefit from the coercive order. Furthermore, because the minority is not absolutely wrong, the coercive order must be constructed in such a way that the minority will not be rendered entirely without rights and itself can become the majority at any time. This is the actual meaning behind the political system we call democracy. Its opposition to absolutism is only possible, because it constitutes the expression of a political relativism.

The eighteenth book of the Gospel of John recounts an event in the life of Jesus. This account, which is simple and lapidary in its naiveté, belongs to one of the greatest literary descriptions, which the world has ever produced. Without intending to do so, it also has become a tragic symbol for relativism and democracy.

The story is set at the time of Easter, when Jesus is brought before Pilate, the Roman governor, under the charge of claiming to be the son of God and the king of the Jews. Pilate asks Jesus, who in the Roman's eyes must seem like a poor fool, ironically: "So you are a king?"[2] Filled with the greatest earnestness and the fervor of his divine mission, Jesus answers: "You say I am a king. For this I was born, and for this I came into the world, to testify to the truth. Everyone who belongs to the truth listens to my voice." Then, Pilate, this man who belongs to an old culture that has grown tired and, hence, skeptical, says: "What is truth?" And because he does not know what truth is and—as a Roman—is accustomed to think democratically, Pilate appeals to the People and conducts a vote. He goes out to the Jews, according to the Gospel, and says to them: "I find no case against him. But you have a custom that I release someone for you at the Passover. Do you want me to release for you the King of the Jews?" The vote goes against Jesus. Then they all cried out again and said: "Not this man, but Barabbas!" But the chronicler adds: "Now Barabbas was a bandit."

Believers—political believers—may object that precisely this example argues against, rather than for, democracy. This objection must be granted, but only under one condition: that these believers are as certain about their political truth, which they will enforce with violence if necessary, as the Son of God was about his.

NOTES

1. The connection between a metaphysical worldview and a commitment to autocracy is readily evidenced by the history of ideas. In his superb essay "Demokratie und Weltanschauung" (*Zeitschrift für öffentliches Recht*, vol. 2, p. 701ff.), Adolf Menzel has already shown that in classical philosophy all notable metaphysicians favor an autocratic politics; this includes Heraclitus and Plato (who in this particular regard must be viewed as more of a metaphysician than as an idealist—two designations which need not necessarily coincide). The sophists, meanwhile, link their natural-philosophical empiricism and relativism to a fight for democracy. Aristotle occupies epistemologically and ethically a middle position between the two. The imposing body of metaphysical thought of medieval scholasticism cannot be systematically separated from its autocratic politics. The organization of human society is conceptualized as a universal monarchy—with the emperor or the Pope as its head—because this organization is thought to be analogous with God's rule over the world. See, in this regard, my work *Die Staatslehre des Dante Alighieri* (1905). Spinoza, whose pantheism must be understood as the transition from metaphysics to an empirical understanding of nature, is a democrat, while the metaphysician Leibnitz with his [theory of a] preordained, God-given harmony consequently favors autocracy.

Kant occupies a unique position. His system is usually referred to as "idealism" and contrasted with positivism. This, however, is clearly a mistake. Its thoroughly critical character already makes Kantian idealism particularly positivistic. Transcendental philosophy can only be properly understood as a theory of experience. In the domain of values, too, this philosophy should, when rigorously applied, lead to a rejection of all metaphysical absolutes and to [the adoption of] relativistic positions [*Aufstellungen*]. But as much as the anti-metaphysical and, thus, positivistic character of Kantian natural philosophy is emphasized, so it is customary to contrast sharply the ethics and political thought of Kant with a relativistic-skeptical attitude; and this view is unquestionably corroborated by Kant's own words. Kant's ethical-political system is altogether metaphysically oriented, and his practical philosophy with its conservative-monarchical theory of state and law necessarily leans toward absolute values (see, in this regard, my work "Die philosophischen Grundlagen der Naturrecht-slehre und des Rechtspositivismus" in *Vorträge der Kant-Gesellschaft*, no. 31, 1928, p. 75f.).

His critical system of pure reason, however, makes cognition [*Erkenntnis*] a continual, never-ending process and relegates truth to the realm of infinity. Hence, truth is rendered just as unattainable here as it is by skepticism. Because cognition can never fully grasp its object, the concern with the object of cognition is replaced in Kant's philosophy by the concern with the method of cognition; indeed, these two concerns become virtually identical. Kantianism has been heavily criticized for this emphasis on methodology, this privileging of the concern with method. Are we here not compelled to draw the parallel to a political disposition, which, instead of concerning itself with the right content of the social order, asks about the way in which or the method according to which that order is generated?

2. [The translation of the biblical text is taken from the *New Revised Standard Version Bible* (Division of Christian Education of the National Council of the Churches of Christ in the U.S.A., 1989).]

Name Index

About the Author and Editors

Hans Kelsen (1881–1973) was an influential jurist and legal philosopher, teaching in Vienna, Geneva, and in the later portion of his life at Harvard University and the University of California at Berkeley. He has been regarded as one of the most important legal scholars of the twentieth century, and the Hans Kelsen Institute (established in 1971 in Austria) as well as the more recently founded Hans Kelsen Research Center at the University of Freiburg honor his legacy to this day.

Nadia Urbinati, the Kyriakos Tsakopoulos Professor of Political Theory and Hellenic Studies at Columbia University, is a political theorist who specializes in modern and contemporary political thought and the democratic and antidemocratic traditions. She co-chaired the Columbia University Faculty Seminar on Political and Social Thought and founded and chaired the Workshop on Politics, Religion and Human Rights.

Carlo Invernizzi Accetti is a political theorist, author, and expert in the study of international democracy, and democratic history.